More Praise for *Leadership by Example*

"Dr. Chopra's book is a guide for future leaders. Among the many important points he makes is the importance of listening. As I have learned, a leader surrounds himself with good people—not yes-men—and listens to what they have to say. More potential leaders have failed because they were deaf to advice than for any other reason."

—Col. Jack Jacobs (Ret.), Medal of Honor recipient and NBC military analyst

"Thoroughly inspiring and motivating. Challenging the convention that to be a leader you need to have followers, the book very effectively aspires to uncover the greatness in EVERY individual. In an interesting narrative that is loaded with excellent quotes, Dr. Chopra has very clearly laid out the underlying principles that define leaders. I would recommend reading the book over and over again periodically to be constantly reminded of the qualities that each of us can develop to bring out the leader in us."

—Zunaira Munir, managing director of Strategize Blue

"Sanjiv Chopra's book is a layman's inspiration to leadership. He shows that leadership is not rabble-rousing. It is not just Mark Antony holding forth with the dead body of Caesar by his side. It is a multidimensional energy that also requires fever, passion, and the will to achieve, whatever one's vocation. In a truly inspirational style, Sanjiv gently guides you over ten commanding leadership steps. If you can catch the infection of his passion and his fever, leadership will surely come your way. As someone who has had the privilege of leading a 65,000-strong police force of India's capital city of Delhi, I learned my leadership skills on the job. I wish Sanjiv's book was with me in those days. Bravo, Sanjiv, for a truly path-breaking book."

—**Vijay Karan, former commissioner of police, Delhi, India, and former director of the Central Bureau of Investigation, India**

"Leadership is a tremendous asset, but conceptualizing and undertaking it has always been somewhat elusive. Sanjiv Chopra clearly spells out easy and time-tested steps for anyone who aspires to be a great leader to follow. This is a most timely book—very much needed to fill the void in leadership at all levels and in all fields in our rapidly changing global world." —**Desh Deshpande, founder of the Deshpande Center for Technological Information at MIT**

"In all my years in academic medicine, the most important lecture I have ever had the pleasure of attending was 'The 10 Tenets of Leadership,' by Professor Sanjiv Chopra. Now available in hard copy, it is a must-read that illustrates how we all can be leaders in our own areas of endeavor, thereby making the world a much better place."

—**Melvin E. Clouse, M.D., Deaconess Professor of Radiology at Harvard Medical School**

Leadership
by Example

Leadership
by Example

The Ten Key Principles of All Great Leaders

Dr. Sanjiv Chopra
with David Fisher

THOMAS DUNNE BOOKS
St. Martin's Press
New York

THOMAS DUNNE BOOKS.
An imprint of St. Martin's Press.

www.thomasdunnebooks.com
www.stmartins.com

ISBN 978-0-312-59490-9 (hardcover)
ISBN 978-1-250-01305-7 (e-book)

First Edition: May 2012

10 9 8 7 6 5 4 3 2 1

I dedicate this book to my wife, Amita Rani, who has nurtured and led our family with dignity, strength, and passion.

And who inspires me in countless ways.

CONTENTS

ACKNOWLEDGMENTS

Writing this book has been a remarkably delightful and rewarding journey. Over the past several years, I've had innumerable discussions about leadership with colleagues, mentors, friends, and family. All of these treasured experiences have shaped and influenced my own concepts of leadership. Beyond this, I've had much time to reflect on my childhood growing up in India and on the four decades that I've lived in the United States. I've also had the privilege of traveling to ninety countries in the world, where I've met and learned from so many gifted and accomplished individuals.

Undoubtedly the most influential people in my

life were my parents, Krishan and Pushpa Chopra. Their life and work left an enduring legacy. In this book, the reader will come across some inspiring stories about them and how while growing up I learned many important life lessons.

In my early childhood and formative years, while a student at St. Columba's High School in New Delhi, My older brother, Deepak, and I stayed with my uncle, Rattan Chacha, and aunt, Karna Auntie. During our many dinner conversations, Deepak and I learned about philosophy, poetry, different world religions, classical music, Shakespeare and Tennyson, Tagore and Swami Vivekananda, ancient and modern history. We were regaled with fascinating stories about great leaders like Mahatma Gandhi and Sir Winston Churchill on many an occasion. Deepak was at a young age a voracious reader and debater. He and I had many a competition regarding historical facts, spelling, and the meaning of words and alliterations. Deepak's singular asset then and now is that he has never had any boundaries. Today he is a prolific author and speaker. He and I are very close as brothers. I am grateful to him for the encouragement and support that he has given to me in my quest and passion to make a positive difference.

The dinner conversations have continued over the years, now with the added and often charming insights of my wife, Amita, my children, Priya, Kanika, Sarat, and Bharat, and my granddaughters, Aanya and Mira. From them, I regularly hear engaging stories about life and leadership, and for that I am ever grateful.

To my many friends—my chosen family—all I can say is thank you so much for being who you are and for being there. It has been a joy and a privilege to celebrate with you occasions big and small.

In my thirty-year academic career at Harvard Medical School, my thoughts, my work, my convictions, and my goals have been shaped immeasurably by my senior distinguished colleagues: Doctors Eugene Braunwald, Arthur Sasahara, Elihu Schimmel,

Raymond Koff, Raj Goyal, Daniel Federman, Peter Banks, Jerry Trier, Joseph Martin, Jeffrey Flier, Robert Glickman, Robert Moellering, Mark Zeidel, and Tom LaMont. They have served as amazing mentors and "packed my parachute" on so many occasions.

I wish to express my sincere appreciation and gratitude to Ivan Kronenfeld and Frank Weimann, who have been immensely supportive. Thomas Dunne and Peter Joseph have been invaluable with their advice and encouragement. I cherish their friendship. David Fisher has been there all along checking and rechecking many of the facts of the stories that will resonate for the readers. David, I am indebted to you for your keen eye and exceptional work in researching some of the stories and double-checking all of the facts.

I am extremely grateful to Donna Abbott, my executive assistant, who has steadfastly worked with me for more than a quarter century. As an esteemed colleague, she has deftly organized and prioritized my workday and adroitly helped me navigate myriad challenges.

David Fisher would also like to acknowledge those leaders in his life, beginning, of course, with his wife, Laura Stevens, whose passion for the health and welfare of others continues to be an inspiration. He would also note that during the preparation of this book, St. Martin's Press's Thomas Dunne Books celebrated its twenty-fifth anniversary, during which time Tom has established himself as an industry leader by publishing a remarkable array of books, ranging from important political opinion to great entertainment. David would also like to acknowledge his sister, Bette Glenn, who under difficult circumstances provided the leadership necessary to raise two fine men, Andrew Glenn and Matt Glenn.

Howard Gardner wrote that great leaders provide leadership in two principal ways: through the stories they tell and through the kind of lives they lead.

INTRODUCTION

I imagine most of you have looked up into the sky and marveled at the sight of a flock of migrating birds flying in V formation. It is quite a beautiful sight. Each bird keeps its place behind the leader, twisting and turning through the air as the leader does. Following without the slightest squawk. It's much easier to be a follower than a leader. Scientists have proven that birds in the formation expend much less energy than the leader. It's easy to be a follower when someone up ahead is cutting down the wind resistance for you.

But what few people know is that this formation has no single leader. One bird flies at the point until it tires, and then it drops back and is replaced by another. During the long migration most of the birds have both the opportunity and the responsibility to become the leader of the formation.

Our lives are similar. Very few of us are leaders all of the time and in everything we do, but all of us can become the leader for a certain time, in specific situations. Maybe it's not surprising that the majority of us do not think of ourselves as leaders. In fact, as children we're taught to be followers: we even play games like Follow the Leader, in which there is only one leader but many followers. As you begin reading this, I'd like you to pause for just one moment and try to count the number of times in the last day that you've been a leader. Literally, pause and think about it. And while you're answering, remember that it is possible to lead at many different levels: in a committee, in your business environment or at a social club, maybe at your religious institution or the Little League or your university or, most important, in your own life in ways that resonate uniquely for you.

True leaders simply move forward
doing what they believe is correct
and what resonates for them, often without
knowing or even being concerned if there
is anyone following.

It's the definition of leadership that confuses many people. There is the belief that to be a leader you must have followers, and, surprisingly, that isn't completely accurate. Leaders take charge by virtue of their actions and decisions; others choose to follow. True leaders simply move forward doing what they believe is correct and what resonates for them, often without knowing or even being concerned if anyone is following. For example, in 1989 a nine-year-old girl living in Nashville, Tennessee, named Melissa Poe saw an episode of the inspirational television program *Highway to Heaven,* in which the leading angel, played by Michael Landon, traveled a quarter century into the future to show what the world would be like if we didn't begin to deal seriously with our environmental problems. It was a cold, harsh world devoid of beauty. Melissa took this message to heart and began by taking a number of actions: she recycled, planted trees, educated her friends, and even wrote letters to newspapers and politicians, including the president of United States,

George H. Bush. In response, the president sent her a pleasant letter urging her to stay in school and not to use drugs.

Melissa eventually founded an organization called Kids for a Clean Environment. Her first club had six members. Remember, this was before young people had easy access to the Internet. To spread the word she picked up the phone and called billboard companies, asking them to donate advertising space. Eventually her letter to President Bush was posted on 250 billboards and she was invited to appear on the *Today Show*. From the determination shown by one young person, KIDS F.A.C.E. has grown to become the world's largest environmental youth organization. It now has more than 300,000 members in 2,000 club chapters in 15 countries, and, in addition to raising environmental awareness, KIDS F.A.C.E. members have distributed and planted more than one million trees.

When Melissa Poe started out she had no intention of becoming a leader; she simply wanted to

If I ask you to conjure up images of people you consider to be great leaders from the pages of history, from ancient times right to our contemporary time, who would come to mind? Whose stories fire your imagination?

make the world a better place. Few people set out knowingly to become leaders; rather, they see a need and find a way of dealing with it, and often others choose to follow their example.

The topic of leadership has fascinated me for as far back as I can remember. To most people of the world Mahatma Gandhi is a legend, but for me, growing up in India in the 1950s, he was revered as a saintly person who had wrought us our freedom from the mighty British with the sheer force of his determination and dedication to truth. I can still hear my parents and grandparents speaking of Gandhi with awe. And I wondered, how could one man, who so often looked frail, make such a tremendous difference in the lives of so many millions of people? In school we studied his life, and for the first time I began asking the questions: What makes an effective leader? How can one lead in both simple and grand ways in their everyday lives? What are the attributes of leadership? And what can we learn by listening to the stories about great leaders like Gandhi?

If I ask you to conjure up images of people you consider to be great leaders from the pages of history, from ancient times right to our contemporary time, who would come to mind? Whose stories fire your imagination? Who are those individuals you most admire? Most people, when asked to identify the great leaders, usually respond by naming historic political and military leaders and perhaps some of the better-known businessmen. The stories of their lives resonate. What is it we learn from those stories? The question becomes, more specifically, how can you, in your everyday life, develop some of the same qualities of leadership that these people have demonstrated?

For three decades Howard Gardner, the Hobbs Professor of Cognition and Education at the Harvard Graduate School of Education, has championed the GoodWork Project. According to Professor Gardner, good work has three essential attributes: it is skilled, it is moral or ethical, and it is meaningful. These qualities are often found in leaders. Gardner has talked and written at length about leadership.

In *Leading Minds: An Anatomy of Leadership,* he wrote that great leaders provide leadership in two principal ways: through the stories they tell and through the kind of lives they lead.

The lives of great leaders—men like Abraham Lincoln, Winston Churchill, and Nelson Mandela—are infused by their passion and sense of purpose. Their courage and accomplishments become legendary tales. The stories of their good works are told and retold by the people they inspire, and then they're told by historians. They leave an everlasting legacy and often influence our world culture and our way of thinking. Books are written about them, documentaries and movies are made, often little children learn about them in school and sometimes portray them in biographical plays. These stories resonate with people throughout the world, and they do so for a long, long time. And that way the lessons of leadership taught by St. Peter, Alexander the Great, Joan of Arc, Galileo, and certainly America's founding fathers, men like Thomas Jefferson,

Benjamin Franklin, and George Washington, continue to have a profound effect on all of us. You don't have to be British to appreciate the extraordinary leadership of Winston Churchill or Indian to remain in awe of Mahatma Gandhi's principles and inspirational leadership. And from all of these people we can identify those elements of leadership that we can apply to our own lives, to make our lives better, to improve the lives of those people who matter to us, and to make a positive contribution to the world.

I like to use mnemonics; a mnemonic is a word or phrase used to help remind us of something larger. For example, "Every good boy does fine" helps people remember that the notes of the musical treble clef are E, G, B, D, and F. The last name of the legendary business leader Lee Iacocca also is a mnemonic standing for "I am Chairman of Chrysler Corporation (of) America." And I use a mnemonic to describe what I believe are the salient qualities inherent in leadership.

The word "leadership" is defined simply as "exhibiting the skills of a leader" or "demonstrating the ability to lead," but in fact its meaning is substantially more than that. Within the word "leadership" can be found the ten letters that spell out the unique attributes exhibited by leaders—the singular qualities that set them apart and that offer lessons from which we can learn.

The letter L, for example, reminds me that leaders must listen well. Good leaders hear the words of the world around them. They listen with both heart and soul and understand what needs to be done. The E stands for the amazing empathy and compassion that many of them demonstrate, the ability to understand and relate to the needs of others—to be in their shoes and feel compelled to take action. A is for the attitude, invariably upbeat and courageous, that draws other people to them and engages their support. The D reminds us that leaders have great dreams and are decisive; they dream of what is possible, but they also are able to make the difficult decisions that are absolutely necessary for success. The

"Leadership" is a simple but powerful word, and by examining it we are reminded of the qualities each us needs to become a leader in our own life.

letter E points out that great leaders are effective; their words may be inspirational, but their actions drive positive change. The R is for "resilient." A great leader often is a risk taker, someone who refuses to accept defeat or the status quo after those first few attempts and will try again and again until a goal is achieved. The S represents the sense of purpose we see in great leaders, who pursue their vision selflessly. The H always reminds me that leaders have humility—and in addition they also have that important quality of humor. They are likable—that's part of the reason we can identify with them, and why we follow them. The I in the leadership mnemonic stands for "integrity." Certainly being a leader requires both integrity, the ability to stand for meaningful principles, and also imagination. Leaders often have wild, improbable ideas and the imagination to believe that they can find the means to accomplish their goals. And finally P; leaders have people skills, they adhere to their principles—and they pack the parachutes of other people, which is a metaphor for mentoring.

"Leadership" is a simple but powerful word, and by examining it we are reminded of the qualities each us needs to become a leader in our own life.

While my journey to an understanding of and great appreciation for the qualities of leadership started early in my life, it was only after I became the Faculty Dean for Continuing Education for Harvard Medical School and was privileged to lead an amazing department that I began to seriously study the techniques of effective leadership. I read hundreds of books on the subject, from biographies of great men to straightforward business books; I attended several courses on the subject; I found opportunities to discuss it with my colleagues around the country and the globe. These individuals included the most brilliant clinicians and scientists and even Nobel laureates. Over the years I began to formulate my own ideas about leadership. I reflected long and hard, wrote down those ideas, and from those notes emerged a lecture on leadership.

I've been privileged to lecture about these ten tenets of leadership for a number of years now as a keynote speaker throughout the United States and in a dozen countries abroad. I've delivered this address to literally tens of thousands of people, many of them my colleagues in the field of medicine but many more of them professionals from an extraordinary variety of other fields. The response has been most gratifying, whether I've given the talk to fifty people or eight thousand. A question that I have been invariably asked is, "Dr. Chopra, do you have a book on this? We would love to share this with our colleagues and our children to inspire them with the wonderful stories you weave into your talk." Quite often, days or weeks or even months after the talk, people will write to me or call me to tell me that they remember the talk, that they were inspired by it and that they have integrated a number of these tenets into their lives and shared them with the people that matter most to them. They tell me they feel they are leading in much more effective ways now.

It is my hope that these stories will resonate with you, and enable you to incorporate the tenets of leadership into your own everyday life. And carry them with you on your leadership journey.

Listen a hundred times, ponder a
thousand times—speak once.
—Turkish proverb

I

LISTENING

Dr. James O'Toole, the Daniels Distinguished Chair of Business Ethics at the University of Denver's Daniels College of Business and the bestselling author of eighteen books, has become well known for his work in understanding corporate culture and the traits of leadership. "The true leader is a listener," he wrote. "The leader listens to the ideas, needs, aspirations and wishes of the followers and then within the context of his or her own well developed system of beliefs responds to these in the appropriate fashion."

Leadership begins with listening. In order to move forward you have to know where you are beginning, and that requires the ability to listen. Not just hear, but really listen. For many people that is not an easy thing to do. They are so excited about expressing their own thoughts and ideas that they don't take the time to actually listen to what other people are saying.

It probably won't surprise anyone to learn that the number-one source of quotes is the Bible, the second most quoted source is the Bard, William Shakespeare. And the third may well be Mr. or Mrs. Anonymous. There is a wonderful Turkish proverb that reminds us to "Listen a hundred times, ponder a thousand times—speak once."

A former major league baseball player and scout named John Young grew up in the decaying section of Los Angeles known as South Central. That neighborhood had once sent a stream of African-American athletes to the major leagues, but by the early 1980s that flow had stopped. Young wondered why and started speaking to members of the community. He listened carefully to their answers. He was told that kids in that area between the ages of thirteen and sixteen quit playing baseball because after Little League there were no organized programs for them. This caused them to turn to other sports—but also to drugs and gangs. As Young learned, the same thing was happening in inner cities throughout the United States. So with little money and few resources, Young founded a program that he named RBI, Reviving Baseball in Inner Cities. From coast to coast volunteers began building baseball fields in vacant lots. Eventually major league baseball got excited about the concept and became a primary sponsor of the program. Today, in 200 American cities more than 200,000 boys and girls are participating in RBI programs. While Young used the lure of baseball to bring kids into RBI he expanded beyond the fields of dreams to include year-round educational programs, peer mentoring, and even vocational training. John Young had no special organizational skills when he founded RBI, but he recognized a problem in his community, asked questions and listened carefully to the answers, and then set out to build a program that would teach kids the skills they needed to succeed in baseball and, much more important, in life.

Leadership absolutely requires a respectful exchange of information, and that means listening as well as talking. The legendary corporate executive Lee Iacocca, who created some of the most successful models in automotive history while at Ford and then transformed Chrysler, which was on the edge of bankruptcy, into an industry leader, once lamented, "I only wish I could find an institute that teaches people how to listen. Business people need to listen at least as much as they need to talk."

The legendary physician and author Oliver Wendell Holmes Sr. was known as one of the most provocative public speakers in the nation, but even he appreciated the importance of listening, reminding people that "It is in the province of knowledge to speak, and it is the privilege of wisdom to listen." And it was Abraham Lincoln who gave us a very

He gave me three pieces of advice
when I became provost:
"Listen, listen and listen."
—Susan Hockfield, president of MIT,
on Richard Levin, president of
Yale University

important reason to simply stop talking and listen, pointing out, "It is better to be silent and be thought a fool than to speak up and dispel all doubt."

Ironically, listening is a skill that often has to be learned and practiced. And for some people, that's difficult. In fact, the actress and playwright Anna Deavere Smith was hired by Yale University to teach its medical students and by New York University to teach its law students the art of listening. As she told them, "Listening is not just hearing what someone tells you word for word. You have to listen with a heart. It is very hard work."

In his acceptance speech in November 2008, the newly elected president, Barack Obama, told a huge crowd that "I will listen to you—especially when we disagree." And later he added, "As Lincoln said in his first inaugural address, to a nation far more divided than ours, 'We are not enemies but friends. Though passion may have strained, it must not break our bonds of affection.' And to those Americans whose support I have yet to earn, I may not have won your vote tonight, but I hear your voices. I need your help."

The president of Yale University, Richard Levin, has become renowned for his ability to nurture academic leaders. When his provost, Susan Hockfield, was appointed president of MIT, she admitted, "He gave me three pieces of advice when I became provost: 'Listen, listen and listen.'" And Levin himself said, "Listening is the first rule of managing."

When we talk about listening as the key to leadership, clearly we mean more than the spoken word. Jack Welch earned a reputation as General Electric's chairman as one of America's most innovative and effective leaders, and he was particularly vocal about listening to new ideas. He wondered why some executives would spend a considerable amount of effort and money to assemble a great workforce—and then refuse to listen to those same people. He believed that the best thing he could do was listen with respect to those people he had hired. In fact, he created a culture at GE where people were rewarded for thinking outside the box and coming up with innovative ideas. And even when an idea failed, even if it cost the company millions of dollars, he still rewarded those people. When asked about that he said, "It is a badge of honor to get good ideas from someone else."

Be kind whenever possible.

It is always possible.

—His Holiness, the Dalai Lama

2

EMPATHY

The second attribute of great leaders is that they have empathy and compassion. And by that I mean that they understand what another person is feeling and often it moves them to take action. There is no doubt that to be a leader you have to be able to relate both intellectually and emotionally to other people.

In May 2009 we had the privilege at the Harvard Medical School of having his Holiness, the Dalai Lama, as the keynote speaker for a course on meditation and psychotherapy. The Dalai Lama has led Tibet's government in exile since fleeing his country in 1959 following the Chinese occupation. Since then he has preached a message of nonviolence and religious harmony, for which he was awarded the Nobel Peace Prize in 1989. He is truly the embodiment of compassion, tranquility, and wisdom and in his Harvard lecture spoke at great length about those subjects. "Be kind whenever possible," he once said, and then added, "It is always possible." I wonder, is there a better definition of compassion than that? He also once noted, "If you want others to be happy, practice compassion. If you want to be happy, practice compassion."

In 1975 twenty-nine-year old Robbie Donno was working in his family's refuse-collection business on Long Island when he read a story in the Rotary Club magazine about a young girl in Uganda who had been attacked by animals and left horribly disfigured. The Rotary in Kampala was asking members around the world for medical assistance. The story touched Robbie's heart. Although he had never gotten involved in anything like this before, he eventually was able to convince St. Francis Hospital of Manhasset to donate its services. Fortunately, others had already aided

The Talmud tells us that compassion is
the highest form of wisdom.

that young girl—but Robbie was told by the Rotary Club in Uganda that another child there was desperately ill and needed open-heart surgery to survive. St. Francis agreed to perform the operation, and the completely volunteer organization that has become known as the Gift of Life was born. Since that time more than twelve thousand children from around the world with life-threatening heart problems have received the operations and care they needed. The Gift of Life is currently in the process of working with local businessmen to open regional cardiac clinics to provide expanded care for children.

Empathy has no boundaries. The Talmud, which is a rich source of traditional Jewish law and customs, tells us that compassion is the highest form of wisdom.

The Buddha preached kindness and empathy and was called the Compassionate One. The prophet Muhammad said, "No man is a true believer unless he desireth for his brother that which he desireth for himself."

Empathy and compassion are timeless,
and we can find extraordinary examples
of them at any time in history.

All of us know the name Florence Nightingale, a name that has become synonymous with offering care and compassion to those in need, but few people actually know her amazing story. Florence Nightingale founded the modern nursing profession in London more than 150 years ago. But by that time she had already transformed the practice of medicine. In 1854 she took thirty-eight volunteer nurses on a harrowing journey across Europe to Turkey to treat soldiers wounded in the Crimean War. Her life, her journey and work became front-page news in England; the *Times* of London called her "The Lady with the Lamp," and wrote about her, "She is a 'ministering angel' without any exaggeration in these hospitals, and as her slender form glides quietly along each corridor, every poor fellow's face softens with gratitude at the sight of her. When all the medical officers have retired for the night and silence and darkness have settled down upon those miles of prostrate sick, she may be observed alone, with a little lamp in her hand, making her solitary rounds."

Florence Nightingale may well have been the first person to practice evidence-based medicine. In the hospitals in Turkey she found the very worst hygienic conditions and eventually she realized that many soldiers were dying not from their injuries, but rather from infections caused by unsanitary conditions. She proved it by displaying pie charts that supported her argument and began spreading the gospel of hygiene and hand washing. By improving living conditions in hospitals she saved countless lives. Today there are three medical schools in Turkey named in her honor.

Empathy and compassion are timeless, and we can find extraordinary examples of them at any time in history. I have a colleague, Dr. Paul Farmer, who is a professor of medicine at Harvard Medical School, a medical anthropologist, and serves as a consultant in infectious diseases. The Pulitzer Prize–winning author Tracy Kidder wrote a wonderful book about him entitled *Mountains Beyond Mountains, the Quest of Dr. Paul Farmer; A Man Who Would Cure the World,* which recounts the inspiring story of Dr. Farmer's lifelong efforts to build a hospital in Haiti's central plateau and bring desperately needed healthcare to the impoverished people of that region.

In 2009 Dr. Farmer was named head of Harvard Medical School's Department of Global Health and Social Medicine. He succeeded his friend and colleague Dr. Jim Yong Kim, another inspirational leader, who in 2006 was named by *Time* one of the one hundred most influential people in the world. Paul Farmer and Jim Kim, along with several colleagues, founded Partners in Health in 1987 to bring medical care to Haiti, and that organization subsequently spread to several other countries. Within a decade Partners in Health was treating more than one thousand Haitian patients every day, as well as fighting tuberculosis among prisoners in Moscow and people living in the slums of Peru. In 1993, Paul Farmer was awarded the John D. and Catherine T. MacArthur "genius award" for his seminal and humanitarian work.

The idea that some lives matter less than others is the root of all that's wrong with the world.
—Dr. Paul Farmer, professor of medicine at Harvard Medical School

Jim Kim, who was named president of Dartmouth College in 2009, once said about his relationship with Farmer, "Paul and I are brothers; we simply happen to have different mothers."

I think it would be fair to say that it is their ability to empathize with people in need that has led Paul, Jim, and all their colleagues to devote so much of their own lives and medical skills to aid others. Paul's philosophy is quite simple. "The idea that some lives matter less than others is the root of all that's wrong with the world." Many years ago he saw a billboard in Haiti with a message that has stayed with him for decades. "The only true nation is humanity."

It would be impossible to even guess how many lives Paul has saved through his work. One of his earliest patients was a Haitian man dying from AIDS. The man was emaciated, barely more than a sack of bones. He was so weak he needed assistance simply to sit up on his bed. Like so many others who came before him, not only was there no help for him, there was no hope. There was nothing special or unique about this man; he wasn't famous or rich, he had no talents that attracted attention to him. But he was a human being and he was suffering. And his suffering was more than Paul could bear. So he and Jim Kim took an empty suitcase to the pharmacy of the Brigham and Women's Hospital in Boston and sweet-talked the pharmacists into filling it with $93,000 worth of anti-retroviral drugs. They took that suitcase to Haiti and treated this patient, giving him both help and hope. In this wonderful situation it worked, the patient survived—and a few years later became the proud father of a beautiful young girl.

The irony with a person like Paul Farmer, so devoted to helping others, is that he neglected his own health and did not take the appropriate precautionary vaccines. One night several years ago at Brigham and Women's Hospital, Paul was making rounds, seeing patients with infectious diseases, when one of his fellows noticed how sickly he looked. "Dr. Farmer," she asked, "Is something wrong?"

Of course, Paul refused to admit that he didn't feel well. He had patients to care for, people who needed his help. "I'm fine," he said, "I need to finish rounds."

The fellow felt Paul's forehead. He had a burning fever. A few hours later Paul almost collapsed and was admitted to the medical service. They immediately started an intravenous line and ordered blood tests. Paul Farmer's first reaction was not about his own health, but rather his patients. He thought, "Oh my God, I have drug-resistant tuberculosis and I've exposed hundreds of patients around the world to it."

That turned out not to be true. What he did have was acute hepatitis A, a potentially dangerous disease that in this instance almost led to acute liver failure. In fact, for a time it appeared he was going to need a liver transplant. Fortunately, he recovered completely.

Paul Farmer with his humility and humanitarian work continues to be a beacon of inspiration to countless others.

Feeling sorry or sympathetic for someone else is a universal emotion; I suspect most of us have empathized with someone in the last day or so—but a leader will take that feeling and translate it into a positive action. Leonard Greene, a member of the National Inventors Hall of Fame and the founder of Safe Flight Instrument Corporation, invented several of the common warning systems that have made worldwide aviation safe. His inventions, including the stall warning and wind-shear warning, are used on more than two-thirds of all the airplanes in the world. In 1981 Leonard got a call from a friend, a commercial pilot named Patricia Blum. While battling cancer Blum had learned first hand how expensive and difficult it could be for a patient to travel around the country to receive the necessary treatment. She lived close to an airport and noticed how often corporate flights were taking off with empty seats. She suggested that perhaps cancer patients needing transportation could fill those seats on already-scheduled flights. Leonard Greene certainly empathized with her. In fact, several years earlier his wife had died of cancer. So he immediately responded. Together they founded what has become known as the Corporate Angel Network, a nationwide system that matches cancer patients who need to travel with scheduled corporate flights heading near the patients' destination. Greene actually piloted the very first Corporate Angel flight, as well as the ten thousandth flight. Today 530 of America's leading corporations participate actively in this organization, and since its founding it has arranged more than 35,000 absolutely free flights for cancer patients.

3

ATTITUDE

Great leaders also have a positive attitude, one that is invariably upbeat and optimistic. I am reminded of the classic story of the newspaper reporter who comes upon a construction site. As he stands there a man walks by pushing a wheelbarrow loaded down with bricks. "Excuse me," the reporter asks, "what are you doing?"

The worker responds angrily, "What does it look like I'm doing? I'm carrying a load of bricks on a really hot, muggy day." And then he walks on, shaking his head.

A few minutes later another worker comes by also pushing a wheelbarrow loaded with bricks. But this laborer is actually whistling. The reporter stops him and asks the same question, "What work are you doing?"

This worker smiles. "Me? I'm helping build the most beautiful cathedral in the world."

Now that's a positive attitude. The great inventor Thomas Edison was well known for his positive attitude. Explaining how he worked, he remarked, "If I find 10,000 ways something won't work I haven't failed. I am not discouraged because every wrong attempt discarded is often a step forward." Later he pointed out, "The making of a light bulb was just a 2,000 step process."

In 1914 Thomas Edison's laboratory burned down. That laboratory was priceless, and with it much of his life's work was completely destroyed. When other people offered their condolences, the then-sixty-seven-year-old Edison replied, "All our mistakes are burnt up. Now we can start anew." Three weeks later he successfully delivered the first

The big secret in life is that there is no big secret. Whatever your goal, you can get there if you are willing to work.

—Oprah Winfrey

phonograph, then quickly rebuilt his laboratory, where he worked for another seventeen years.

Few people have expressed a more positive attitude than Oprah Winfrey, who overcame a childhood of poverty and sexual abuse to become one of the most admired persons in the world, a person who has used her fame and wealth to educate, enlighten, and benefit millions of people. As Oprah once told her viewers, "When I look into the future, it's so bright it burns my eyes."

And as she also once remarked, "The big secret in life is that there is no big secret. Whatever your goal, you can get there if you are willing to work."

An upbeat attitude is infectious. A positive attitude can lift the spirits of everyone around you and inspire other people to greatness. Leaders possess an attitude that is upbeat and courageous. The great British statesman and prime minister Sir Winston Churchill once said, "Courage is rightly esteemed the first of human qualities because it is the quality that guarantees all others." It was Churchill's stirring words of defiance during the worst moments of World War II that rallied the Commonwealth behind him. On June 4, 1940, the British army had retreated from the continent in shambles. As Nazi bombers attacked Britain's vulnerable cities night after night and the country prepared for what was believed to be the inevitable invasion, Churchill rallied the nation. Speaking in the House of Commons, he promised, "We shall go on to the end. We shall fight in France. We shall fight on the seas and oceans, we shall fight with growing confidence and growing strength in the air, we shall defend our Island, whatever the cost may be. We shall fight on the beaches. We shall fight on the landing grounds. We shall fight in the fields and in the streets, we shall fight in the hills; We shall never surrender."

Unfortunately, around the world there are countries that lack enlightened leadership, and their citizens are subjugated and live in fear. As Thomas Jefferson wrote, "Enlighten the people generally, and tyranny and oppression of body and mind will vanish like evil spirits at the dawn of day." Great leaders govern with both heart and soul. Conversely, those countries without great leaders, men or women without soul, will not only be ecologically and economically disadvantaged, they will also be spiritually bankrupt. They will emerge from the morass and their shackles only when an enlightened leader emerges.

This is the situation currently in countries like Myanmar, which formerly was known as Burma, as well as North Korea and Iran, where the people are purposefully kept in the dark of tyranny, waiting until a leader will emerge to take them into the light. In 1991 the Burmese politician Aung San Suu Kyi was awarded the Nobel Peace Prize for her efforts to free her country from a brutal dictatorship. She is an amazing woman who has been fighting to bring democracy to her country her entire life; she is the daughter of the man who had led Burma's independence movement from Britain in 1947. He rightfully won the elections but was then assassinated. At an early age Aung San Suu Kyi became a believer in

It is not power that corrupts, but fear. Fear of losing power corrupts those who wield it and fear of the scourge of power corrupts those who are subject to it.

—Aung San Suu Kyi, winner of the Nobel Peace Prize

Gandhi's philosophy of nonviolent resistance to tyranny. After being educated in India and Europe, she returned to Myanmar in 1988 to enter politics. Since then she has spent the majority of her time living under house arrest in Rangoon. The dictatorship running Myanmar wants her to leave the country. In fact, after her husband, who was living in England, was diagnosed with cancer the government offered her a visa to be with him—but she refused to go. She could have left safely and been living a celebrated life in the West. But she believed that if she left her country she would never be permitted to return and that it is her duty to her people to be with them. "It is not power that corrupts," she once said, "but fear. Fear of losing power corrupts those who wield it and fear of the scourge of power corrupts those who are subject to it."

The citation for her Nobel Peace Prize reads, "Aung Suu Kyi became the leader for democratic opposition which employs non-violent means to resist a regime characterized by brutality. Suu Kyi's struggle is one of the most extraordinary examples of civil courage in Asia in recent decades. She has become an important symbol in the struggle against oppression."

Her bravery is extraordinary. In 1989, while leading a march for democracy, she was confronted by soldiers blocking a street. An officer warned her to stop, threatening that his troops would shoot if the marchers attempted to continue their demonstration. In response, Suu Kyi told her supporters to wait, then marched up and through the ranks of the soldiers who were aiming their weapons at her. At the last moment the troops were ordered to lower their rifles. "It seemed much simpler to provide them with a single target than to bring everyone else in," she explained. So Aung Suu Kyi is a person who leads not only with her words, but with her attitude of defiance—and she also is a leader who has great dreams for her nation.

When she finally was released from house arrest in November 2010, her followers were overjoyed and wanted to celebrate. But Aung Suu Kyi was somber and, instead of rejoicing, explained, "I'm not really free until my people are free."

The very essence of leadership is that you have to have a vision. It's got to be a vision you articulate clearly and forcefully on every occasion. You can't blow a weak trumpet.

—Theodore Hesburgh, former president of Notre Dame University

V*ision is the art of seeing things*

invisible to others.

—Jonathan Swift

4

DREAMING

Great leaders have great dreams—and they are decisive. They have a vision of what is possible. Paraphrasing a line from *Back to Methuselah,* by George Bernard Shaw, the U.S. attorney general and presidential candidate Robert F. Kennedy once said, "There are those that look at things the way they are, and ask why? I dream of things that never were, and ask why not." And Father Theodore Hesburgh, the widely respected former president of Notre Dame University, told students there, "The very essence of leadership is that you have to have a vision. It's got to be a vision you articulate clearly and forcefully on every occasion. You can't blow a weak trumpet."

The British satirist Jonathan Swift wrote, "Vision is the art of seeing things invisible to others." But remember that in addition to having a clear and compelling vision, one has to have a road map to achieve that vision. A wise old proverb reminds us, "A vision without a plan is just a dream. A plan without a vision is just drudgery. But a vision with a plan can change the world."

Perhaps no one better articulated the importance of a vision to rally support than Dr. Martin Luther King. Speaking from the steps of the Lincoln Memorial on August 28, 1963, King spoke for seventeen minutes to a crowd estimated at more than two hundred thousand Americans who had marched on Washington in support of the civil rights movement. While most of this speech had been carefully written, as he reached the end he departed from his prepared text and began speaking from his heart:

I still have a dream. It is a dream deeply rooted in the American dream. I have a dream that

one day this nation will rise up and live out the true meaning of its creed: "We hold these truths to be self-evident, that all men are created equal."

I have a dream that one day on the red hills of Georgia, the sons of former slaves and the sons of former slave owners will be able to sit down together at the table of brotherhood. . . .

I have a dream that my four little children will one day live in a nation where they will not be judged by the color of their skin but by the content of their character . . .

I have a dream that one day every valley shall be exalted, and every hill and mountain shall be made low, the rough places will be made plain, and the crooked places will be made straight; and the glory of the Lord shall be revealed and all flesh shall see it together.

But dreams shouldn't be limited to the leaders of nations or movements. All of us need to learn how to pay attention to our dreams. Too many of us easily dismiss our own dreams as impossibilities. As the writer Gloria Steinem cautioned, "Without leaps of imagination, or dreaming, we lose the excitement of possibilities. Dreaming, after all, is a form of planning."

The German writer Johann Goethe once said, "Whatever you can do, or dream you can do, begin it. Boldness has genius, power, and magic in it!"

Sometimes it takes a dreamer to make the dreams of others come true. I have long pointed out that while leaders often have a compelling vision of the future, they also have a clear view of the present. They understand the difficulties of the course they've set, but rather than shrinking from a challenge, they embrace it. Henry David Thoreau advised, "If you have built castles in the air, your work need not be lost. That is where they should be. Now go put the foundations underneath."

In 1980, a seven-year-old Arizona boy name Chris Greicius was diagnosed with leukemia. More than anything else in the world, Chris wanted to become a police officer. When a U.S. customs officer named Tommy Austin heard about Chris from a family friend, he contacted the Arizona Department of Public Safety and with its cooperation arranged for Chris's dream to come true: Chris was flown to police headquarters in the department's helicopter and sworn in as the only honorary patrolmen in state history. He received a custom-tailored uniform and, with help, passed the motorcycle proficiency test—on his battery-operated motorcycle—which allowed him to receive his wings to wear on his uniform. Four days later he died, with his uniform, motorcycle helmet, and Smokey the Bear hat hanging in his hospital room.

The small group of people who had made Chris's wish come true, including Tommy Austin and the DPS officers, saw the joy it had brought him and his family and wondered if they could do the same thing for other sick children. There was nothing unusual or special about these people; most of them worked in law-enforcement agencies. They weren't dreaming about freeing a nation from a dictator or being awarded the Nobel Prize. Their concept was elegant yet powerful in its simplicity: they wanted to fulfill the dreams of children suffering from terrible diseases. A grocery store manager donated the first $35, and the Make-A-Wish Foundation was born to fulfill the wishes of children diagnosed with life-threatening medical conditions. In the next two years this little group was able to grant the wishes of eight more young people. When their story was told on national television, people began calling from all over the country to find out how they could do the same thing in their communities. Currently there are more than sixty-five Make-A-Wish chapters in the United States and another thirty-five around the world. By 2010 this volunteer organization had made wishes come true for almost two hundred thousand children—which have included meeting world-famous celebrities, attending glamorous events, and even "working" as a reporter, a veterinarian, and a pyrotechnician.

The power of dreams should never be underestimated. It's sad but true that most of us at some time put our dreams aside. But there are people who hold fast to their dreams and pursue them no matter how impossible they may seem.

Let me tell you a story about holding on to your dreams. It's the story of a seventeen-year-old high school student in Texas, who was given a homework assignment to write an essay entitled "What I Want to Do When I Grow Up." This young man's father was a stable hand and moved from one horse farm to another. But he was a big dreamer, and he wrote a seven-page essay explaining that his dream was that one day he would own a two-hundred-acre horse farm. He even drew pictures of the stables and wrote about the way he would run his stables and how he would care for his horses with love.

A few days later the teacher returned his essay.

To dare is to lose one's footing momentarily. Not to not dare is to lose oneself.

—Søren Kierkegaard

He'd given him a F. Then he explained why. "The hardest part of life is accepting reality," the teacher said to this young man. "Your dream is completely unrealistic. We live in a small town, and no one here has ever achieved anything like this. But you're an intelligent kid, so I'm going to give you another chance. If you want to write another essay, I'll accept it and be happy to grade it."

The boy went home and thought about it for a few days. And when he returned to school he told his teacher, "You can keep the F. I'll keep my dream."

Twenty-two years later the boy had grown up and become successful. And he was the proud owner of a 172-acre horse farm. He received a letter from his former teacher asking if he could bring his class to the horse farm for a picnic. In the middle of that picnic the teacher stood up and told the entire story to his students. He then turned to his former student and said, "I want to apologize to you. I was a dream stealer. And I will never do that again."

It was the great Victorian British poet, Robert

Browning, who wrote, "Ah, but a man's reach should exceed his grasp. Or what's a heaven for?"

But perhaps it was the Danish philosopher and theologian Søren Kierkegaard who said it best, "To dare is to lose one's footing momentarily. Not to not dare is to lose oneself."

It can't be emphasized enough that leaders have the fortitude and courage to dream, and they remain resolute in pursuit of those dreams. Calvin Coolidge, the thirtieth president of the United States, understood that, explaining, "Nothing in the world can take the place of persistence. Talent will not; nothing is more common than unsuccessful men with talent. Genius will not; unrewarded genius is almost a proverb. Education will not; the world is full of educated derelicts. Persistence and determination alone are omnipotent. The slogan 'Press On' has solved and always will solve the problems of the human race."

When I'm asked to conjure up my own vision of leadership, what invariably comes to mind is the

When I'm asked to conjure up my own vision of leadership, what invariably comes to mind is the image of Mahatma Gandhi and the salt march in 1930. It was this epic journey that awakened an entire nation and sparked India's freedom movement.

image of Mahatma Gandhi and the salt march in 1930. It was this epic journey that awakened an entire nation and sparked India's freedom movement. Natural salt is plentiful in India. It could have been easily collected on the sunbaked beaches, but the British rulers of colonial India had passed a law making it a criminal offense for Indians to pick up that salt for their own use or to sell it. Instead, Indians were forced to purchase imported salt from the British and pay an exorbitant tax on it, a heavy and unjust burden on the average citizen. Gandhi announced he was going to walk 240 miles across India to the ocean, where he would defy the law by picking up Indian salt. If the British soldiers stopped him, he warned, he would not resist. As he wrote to the British leader in India, Viceroy, Lord Irwin, "I cannot intentionally hurt any thing that lives, much less fellow-human beings even though they may do the greatest wrong to me and mine. Whilst therefore I hold British rule to be a curse, I do not intend to harm a single Englishman or any legitimate interest

Gandhi once listed what he considered the seven sins of the world: wealth without work, pleasure without conscience, knowledge without character, commerce without morality, science without humanity, worship without sacrifice, and politics without principle.

he may have in India . . . I regard this tax to be the most iniquitous of all from the poor man's standpoint. As the Independence Movement is essentially for the poorest in the land, the beginning will be made with this evil." This letter announced the beginning of Gandhi's campaign of nonviolent civil disobedience. His march took twenty-three days and attracted the attention of the world. He chose seventy-eight men to march with him on this historic journey, among them were Hindus, Christians, Muslims, and Untouchables, the lowest class of Indian society. The youngest was only sixteen while, at sixty-two years, Gandhi was the oldest. Every day stories about his march appeared on the front pages of newspapers. In each village he passed through throngs of people would join him until, by the time he reached the coastal village of Dandi, his procession was more than two miles long.

Once there, he defied British rule by picking up a small lump of mud salt and boiling it in seawater to produce a pinch of salt. And then he implored other

Indians to do the same thing. Eventually Gandhi as well as an estimated eighty thousand of his followers were arrested. And when British soldiers brutally attacked unresisting marchers in another town and beat them with their clubs, people in America and throughout Europe, as well as women factory workers in London, were captivated and horrified. This was the start of the movement that less than two decades later would result in India's becoming independent. And Gandhi's nonviolent philosophy would become the bedrock of other popular movements throughout the world, especially the civil rights movement in the United States.

Gandhi once listed what he considered the seven sins of the world: wealth without work, pleasure without conscience, knowledge without character, commerce without morality, science without humanity, worship without sacrifice, and politics without principle. To me, these tenets embody the principles of leadership. Great leaders have a work ethic. They have a clear conscience. They have character, they

Be the change you want to see
in the world.

—Gandhi

have morality, they are grounded in humanity, they may make enormous sacrifices—often lifelong sacrifices—and they adhere strongly to their principles.

Mahatma Gandhi easily could have led a much more luxurious life. He was a lawyer admitted to the British bar, his family was well connected to political leaders, and, had he chosen to, he could have had a comfortable existence. Instead, he chose to live simply, almost completely unburdened by possessions. In fact, he spent almost six years of his life in prison for his beliefs, and several times led hunger strikes. When he stayed in Bombay, or Mumbai as it is known now, he lived at the home of a friend and slept on a mattress on the floor. His worldly possessions consisted of little more than a bowl and plate, glasses and slippers, a cotton spinning wheel, and the Bhagavad Gita, the Hindu scripture. His eloquence was electrifying. He once noted, "It is my certain conviction that with every thread I draw I am spinning the destiny of India." His work and life left an indelible imprint on the world. After Gandhi had been assassinated, Albert Einstein said, "Generations to come, it may be, will scarce believe that such a one as this, ever in flesh and blood, walked upon the earth."

Perhaps Gandhi will be most often remembered for the simple advice he gave for leading a good and moral life, "Be the change you want to see in the world."

While great leaders dream, when it is necessary they also can make daring and difficult decisions, but few were more difficult than that facing General Anthony McAuliffe in December 1944. After landing on the beaches of Normandy on June 6 that year, the Allied forces had swept across Europe, forcing the Germans to retreat. But the German army mounted one last massive counterattack, Hitler's final desperate effort to survive, which became known in history as the Battle of the Bulge. The surprised American army was initially overwhelmed. In the French city of Bastogne the 101st Airborne Division was completely surrounded by a much larger German force. German general Walther von Lüttwitz sent an ultimatum to the American commander, General Anthony McAuliffe: "There is only one possibility to save the encircled U.S.A. troops from total annihilation: that is the honorable surrender of the encircled town. In order to think it over a term of two hours will be granted beginning with the presentation of this note. If this proposal should be rejected one German Artillery Corps and six heavy A. A. Battalions are ready to annihilate the U.S.A. troops in and near Bastogne."

General McAuliffe did not need the two hours to make his decision. With the lives of his men at stake his one-word letter in reply has become legend. In his note addressed, "To the German Commander," he wrote, "NUTS!, The American Commander." The Germans attacked, but the valiant 101st proudly rallied behind their leader. The next day the weather cleared sufficiently for the army air force to attack the German supply lines and drop supplies to the beleaguered troops in the city of Bastogne. Three days later General George Patton's Third Army broke through the German ring to relieve McAuliffe's troops and turn the tide of battle.

Making a firm decision is often the most difficult thing a leader can do; lives and careers may be at stake, but great leadership requires it. In fact, as Napoleon said, "Nothing is more difficult, and therefore more precious, than to be able to decide."

Decisiveness is absolutely necessary. T. Boone Pickens, the Texas entrepreneur and businessman who founded Mesa Petroleum, one of the largest independent oil companies in the world, advised, "Be willing to make decisions. That's the most important quality in a good leader. Don't fall victim to what I call the ready-aim-aim-aim syndrome. You must be willing to fire."

In October 1962, President John Kennedy was faced with one of the most difficult decisions in American history when spy planes revealed that the Soviet Union was helping Cuba build bases from which nuclear missiles could be launched against the United States. While many members of Kennedy's cabinet urged him to launch a military attack on Cuba before those bases could be completed, instead Kennedy announced publicly that the United States was initiating a blockade to prevent missiles from being delivered to Cuba and demanded that Soviet leader Nikita Khrushchev dismantle the existing bases. As the Russian ships carrying those missiles sailed toward Cuba and a confrontation with the American fleet, Kennedy told the nation:

[L]et no one doubt that this is a difficult and dangerous effort on which we have set out. No one can foresee precisely what course it will take or what costs or casualties will be incurred . . . But the greatest danger of all would be to do nothing.

The path we have chosen for the present is full of hazards, as all paths are; but it is the one most consistent with our character and courage as a nation and our commitments around the world. The cost of freedom is always high, but Americans have always paid it. And one path we shall never choose, and that is the path of surrender or submission.

With the world on the brink of nuclear war, Khrushchev announced that he would recall the ships and dismantle the launching sites in return for an American pledge not to invade Cuba. Kennedy agreed. A year later the United States removed its own missiles, based in Turkey, which had been aimed at the Soviet Union. Kennedy's decisive stance may have prevented war.

In business, as in politics, failing to make a decision and to take responsibility for it can have disastrous results. Rupert Murdoch, who took one newspaper in Adelaide, Australia, and founded News Corp, now the world's third largest media company, said firmly, "You can't build a strong corporation

Managers are for today.
Leaders are for tomorrow.
—Dipak Jain, former dean of
Northwestern's Kellogg School
of Management

with a lot of committees and a board that has to be consulted at every turn. You have to be able to make decisions on your own."

Both managers and leaders make decisions, but there is a singular difference between the two. I once asked Dipak Jain, then the dean of Northwestern's Kellogg School of Management, how he would define that difference. "It is simple," he replied eloquently, "Managers are for today. Leaders are for tomorrow."

Management is efficiency in climbing the ladder of success; leadership determines whether the ladder is leaning against the right wall.

—Dr. Stephen Covey, the author of The Seven Habits of Highly Effective People

5

EFFECTIVE

D r. Stephen Covey, the author of the influential bestseller *The Seven Habits of Highly Effective People,* once noted, "Management is efficiency in climbing the ladder of success; leadership determines whether the ladder is leaning against the right wall."

Anthony Mayo, a distinguished member of the faculty at the Harvard Business School, and Nitin Nohria, who was appointed dean of that business school in 2010, explained in their book *In Their Time: The Greatest Business Leaders of the Twentieth Century,* "Entrepreneurs create new businesses, managers grow and optimize them and leaders transform them at critical inflection points."

Great leaders are effective. They understand what needs to be done and they do it. Gandhi rallied an entire nation behind him. Peter Drucker, the visionary who, beginning in 1939 and continuing till his death in 2005, wrote thirty-nine books that essentially formed the foundation for modern American business practice, is considered by many people to be the founding father of modern management techniques. Drucker wrote in his 1966 classic, *The Effective Executive,* that the foundation of good leadership is understanding the difference between efficiency and effectiveness. "Efficiency is doing things right; effectiveness is doing the right things. There is surely nothing quite so useless as doing with great efficiency what should not be done at all."

And later he added, "I've seen a great many people who are . . . magnificent at getting the unimportant things done. They have an impressive record of achievement on trivial matters."

Certainly no one understood the value and the

consequences of using words effectively better than Winston Churchill. It was said that for a one-minute speech he would prepare for an hour, and for an hour speech he prepared for ten hours. As a speaker he could galvanize Britain and the world with his words; as a writer he received the Nobel Prize in Literature for his history of World War II. The American general Omar Bradley is reputed to have said of Churchill's ability to rally his nation with his words, "One speech of Sir Winston Churchill has more might than an entire battalion."

President John F. Kennedy, on granting U.S. citizenship to Winston Churchill in 1963, said in tribute, "He mobilized the English language and sent it into battle."

On June 18, 1940, only two weeks after vowing that Britain would never surrender, Churchill once again stood in the House of Commons to address Parliament. France had surrendered and Britain was left alone to face Hitler's seemingly invincible German army. In his most somber tones, Churchill declared:

The battle of Britain is about to begin. Upon this battle depends the survival of Christian civilization. Upon it depends our own British life, and the long continuity of our institutions and our Empire. The whole fury and might of the enemy must very soon be turned on us. Hitler knows that he will have to break us in this island or lose the war. If we can stand up to him, all Europe may be freed and the life of the world may move forward into broad, sunlit uplands.

But if we fail, then the whole world, including the United States, including all that we have known and cared for, will sink into the abyss of a new dark age made more sinister, and perhaps more protracted, by the lights of perverted science. Let us therefore brace ourselves to our duties, and so bear ourselves, that if the British Empire and its Commonwealth last for a thousand years, men will still say, "This was their finest hour."

In addition to Churchill, many of those people we acknowledge today as effective leaders emerged from the cauldron of World War II. Among them were Presidents Franklin Roosevelt, Harry Truman, and Dwight Eisenhower, and military leaders including Generals Douglas MacArthur, George S. Patton, Erwin Rommel, and Charles de Gaulle. Which leads to the complex question, was Adolf Hitler an effective leader? There is no simple answer to that. Hitler clearly was an unusually charismatic man; he was a fiery orator who took control of a great and cultured nation and led it to physical and moral destruction. Hitler's extraordinary ability to appeal to millions of followers was at the heart of the actor-writer Robert Shaw's controversial play and movie, *The Man in the Glass Booth*. At the conclusion a character based loosely on Adolf Eichmann—the bureaucrat who supervised the Holocaust and was later put on trial in Israel—locked himself in a glass booth. And in a whisper he tells the horrified courtroom, "Speaking of love, let me speak to you of my Fuhrer. We loved him. People of Israel, if he had chosen you, you also would have followed."

Provocative words, but I think the question of whether Hitler was a great leader is probably best answered by the Nobel Peace Prize laureate Elie Wiesel, who survived the Holocaust and has done more than anyone else to bring the horrors of the Nazis to the public conscience. In an essay that appeared in *Time* magazine in 1998, he wrote:

Few people of this century have aroused, in their lifetime, such love and so much hate; few have inspired so much historical and psychological research after their death . . .

The fact is that Hitler was beloved by his people—not the military, at least not in the

beginning, but by the average Germans who pledged to him an affection, a tenderness and a fidelity that bordered on irrational. It was idolatry on a national scale. One had to see the crowds who acclaimed him . . . Did they not see the hateful mask that covered his face . . .

His kingdom collapsed after 12 years in a war that remains the most atrocious, the most brutal and the deadliest in the history . . . But when later we evoke the 20th century, among the first names that will surge to mind will be that of a fanatic with a mustache who thought to reign by selling the soul of his people to the thousands of demons of hate and death.

Was Adolph Hitler an effective leader? The deaths of millions and the ruins of his nation would argue strongly against it.

At the conclusion of that war, on May 8, 1945, Victory in Europe Day, Winston Churchill stood on the balcony of Buckingham Palace with the royal family speaking to the thousands of people who had gathered to share this historic day with the man who had rallied his nation. Prime Minister Churchill gave a very short speech. "This is your victory," he said. "It is the victory of the cause of freedom in every land. In all our long history we have never seen a greater day than this. Everyone, man or woman, has done their best . . . Neither the long years, nor the dangers, nor the fierce attacks of the enemy, have in any way weakened the independent resolve of the British nation." And no sooner had Churchill said those first words, "This is your victory," than the crowd below erupted in a great cheer and shouted back, "No. It is yours," and then burst spontaneously into a raucous rendition of "For He's a Jolly Good Fellow."

John Quincy Adams, the sixth president of the United States, said once, "If your actions inspire others to dream more, learn more, do more and become more, you are a leader." No one better exemplifies that than a man named Muhammad Yunus, a professor of rural economics from Bangladesh. In 1976, while teaching at a university, he took his class on a field trip to a nearby village whose residents were barely eking out a living making bamboo stools. To purchase the bamboo they needed for their work, these women were forced to take out small loans from a middleman, loans for which they were being charged as much as 10 percent interest every week. Their profit margin on each bushel of bamboo they purchased was two cents. At that rate these women were going to be indebted for life, but they had no choice. No one else would loan them the few dollars they needed. As Yunus remembered, "I made a list of people who needed just a little bit of money, and when the list was complete, there were forty-two names. The total amount of money they needed was $27. I was shocked."

As the story is told, Muhammad Yunus went to a local bank and asked the bankers why they refused to loan money to the workers at a reasonable interest rate. As he remembered it, the bankers nearly fell over. These women had no credit, the bankers explained, they had nothing to offer for collateral; there was no way to guarantee the bank would ever get its money back.

So the economics professor took this problem into his own hands. Literally. Rather than despairing about the bank, Yunus reached into his own pocket and loaned the forty-two weavers the equivalent of $27. Within a year those forty-two women had repaid the original loan and had established an ongoing business. Yunus discovered that there were many other people like these women in Bangladesh, hardworking people who needed only a few dollars to fund a business or obtain a product that might change their lives. And while none of these people had any collateral to put up, Yunus had faith in mankind. He believed people could be trusted to repay those tiny loans—and so he opened a small bank to make what he called microloans. To make it easier for individuals, he created five member-solidarity groups in which all the members of the group served as coguarantors of the loans.

Muhammad Yunus's Grameen, meaning "village" or "rural" bank, was founded in 1983 based on trust and solidarity. The bank doesn't require any collateral, and borrowers don't have to sign any legal papers. If borrowers can't pay back the loan, the bank doesn't take legal action. The average loan is less than $100. By 2010 the bank had made $9.7 billion in microloans and $8.5 billion had been repaid. There have been almost 8.5 million borrowers, almost all of them women, and the loan recovery rate was 97.3%—the highest of any bank in the world. The bank has 2,564 branches in 81,000 villages and employs 22,500 people and has been almost consistently profitable. It even gives out interest-free loans to beggars and has set up a rudimentary pension system.

Muhammad Yunus has changed the world, one loan at a time, one life at a time. For example, almost 400,000 people have borrowed money from

W here there is no vision,
the people perish.

—King Solomon, Proverbs 29:18

Grameen Bank to buy cell phones. Those cell phones enabled fisherwomen in small villages to send a photograph of their catch directly to the fish merchants at the central market in Dhaka, bypassing the middlemen who would take most of their profits.

In 2006 Yunus and the Grameen Bank were jointly awarded the Nobel Peace Prize. In announcing this award, the Nobel committee wrote, "Muhammad Yunus has shown himself to be a leader who has managed to translate visions into practical action for the benefit of millions of people . . . At Grameen Bank, credit is a cost–effective weapon to fight poverty, and it serves as a catalyst in the overall development of socio–economical conditions of the poor who have been kept outside the banking orbit on the grounds that they are poor and hence not bankable." The microbank concept has spread to more than sixty countries throughout the world, including the United States, and has improved the lives of millions of people.

In Proverbs 29:18 the wise King Solomon warned, "Where there is no vision, the people perish." We need visionary leaders, those people who have the foresight and the ability to open the possibilities of a better future to the world.

Great leaders reflect on key events in their own lives and often focus on a single transformative or magical moment. That event or movement can be, in fact, starkly negative and jolting, and yet it is momentous and from it emerges their laserlike focus and passion to turn a dream into reality. The Buddha once said, "Every life has a measure of sorrow. Sometimes it is this that awakens us." There are people who can take a tragedy and turn it into something of great value. One of these people is Jaime Jaramillo, who is known affectionately throughout the nation of Colombia as Papa Jaime. In 1973, then twenty-eight-year-old Jaime Jaramillo was standing on a street corner in Bogotá. He was a geological engineer who had prospected around the world, a man deeply involved in a difficult business. And as he

Every life has a measure of sorrow.

Sometimes it is this that awakens us.

—The Buddha

waited there he looked across the street and saw a beautiful seven-year-old girl looking back at him. He recognized her immediately as one of the countless orphaned children living on the streets of the city, a child who had absolutely nothing. She smiled at him. Suddenly, a luxury car came slowly around the corner and stopped; someone rolled down a window and tossed a box out into the street, and then the car drove away. It was an empty box, but to that little girl it was a treasure. She ran out into the street to pick it up, beaming with joy, and suddenly a truck roared around the corner and hit her, killing her instantly.

Jaime stood there in shock. Suddenly he knew he had to do something to help these children, but he didn't know how one man could make any difference. There were so many of them. Nevertheless, he began walking the streets of the city at night, talking to children, trying to learn about them. He met a little girl who had been badly burned and asked her to show him where she lived. She took him into the sewers of the city, and there he discovered an entire community of kids living in filthy, dangerous underground sewers.

He began bringing food to them. He bought them presents and once even dressed up as Santa Claus, causing a little boy to ask if he was really Papa Noel, which later led to his nickname, Papa Jaime. He had found his purpose in life. As he once explained, "I felt a huge compassion when a boy jumped on my shoulders and rubbed his face against mine, and then later I realized that he had transferred something yellow onto my face. It was pus from a putrid rat bite. It sounds disgusting, but that boy had no idea how bad his wound was. He had no one in his life who wanted to love him and heal him. My dream was to help heal this boy and all the others like him."

That was the beginning. In the last three decades, Papa Jaime has taken more than thirty thousand children off the streets and out of the sewers of Bogotá, not only saving their lives but helping them escape from extreme poverty. He has provided them housing and food and an opportunity for an educa- tion. And just as importantly, he has shown them that there are people who care about them.

Several years ago I was privileged to meet Papa Jaime at a leadership conference at Northwestern University's esteemed Kellogg School of Manage- ment. He gave a brief speech, no longer than ten minutes, and by the time he had finished people were in tears. When we spoke later he showed me a photograph of a young girl and told me her story. She had been begging outside a fancy restaurant and the owner called the police. In fact, it was not the police who responded, but rather a death squad. They took this girl, put her back in the sewer, and torched her. Somehow she survived, although she had third-degree burns all over her body. With his help, she underwent seventeen plastic surgeries, and then he sent her to the United States. She went to college and has become a computer scientist, and is now married with a child of her own. Papa Jaime showed me other photographs of the young people he has rescued. One photograph I remember showed a young man dressed in tennis whites standing between the tennis legends Pete Sampras and Andre Agassi. He had become a junior tennis champion. Some of the other children he's rescued have become doctors and nurses and teachers. It was incredible. I asked him, "How much of a staff do you have to help you?" He told me he had 150 people. I asked him, "How do you take care of all the expenses? How do you pay for food, schooling, and housing? How can you afford to pay for everything you do?"

"I have a factory," he told me. "It's a bakery and the only thing we make is cookies. I've convinced the restaurants in Bogotá to put a cookie jar next to the cash register. As people are leaving they take a cookie and hopefully drop a few coins or a dollar into the jar." He laughed as he thought about it. "When I proposed that, at first people believed I was naive. They told me it would never work, that we would need to put a padlock on the jar. But I did not believe that, and the money comes to us. We can support about half of all our needs this way."

And what about the other half, I asked? Where does that come from?

Papa Jaime shrugged and said, "Sanjiv, it comes." I didn't understand what that meant, "it comes." And so I asked him again. He responded by telling me a story. "A few years ago I needed forty-five-thousand American dollars to pay some of my bills. I went to a bank, and they couldn't help me. So I went to a second bank, and a third, and each of them turned me down. 'We love you, Papa Jaime,' they told me, 'but you already have loans to us. We can't help you anymore.' As I left the third bank to return to my office, a street woman recognized me. She stopped me and gave me a big hug. 'Are you hungry?' I asked her, and she said yes, she was very hungry. So I brought her with me to my office and offered her some of our cookies with some coffee. As she sat there eating, I began making my phone calls to other banks. And I was turned down by another bank, and then another, but I continued to call. Finally, she asked me, 'How much do you need?' I told her, 'Forty-five-thousand US dollars.' And she said, 'Okay, I'll give it to you.' I laughed to myself, thinking that she meant so well, but clearly she was cuckoo. Then she opened her purse. She had $60,000 US dollars in there. I was stunned beyond astonishment. She explained that her son had sent her the money to buy a house so she could live safely off the streets. She said, 'I don't need it, your children need it. Please take it, no questions asked, and you can return it to me when it is possible.'"

Witnessing the tragic death of one little girl had inspired Papa Jaime to build his organization Niños de Los Andes, which continues to bring light and fulfillment into the lives of children every single day.

6

RESILIENT

Great leaders are resilient; for them failure is often only the first step on a long and arduous journey. There are countless people who emerge as leaders when things are going well, but it is those people who take the reins of leadership to turn failure into success who eventually become our true leaders. Few leaders have proved to be more resilient than Nelson Mandela, who spent twenty-seven years in prison for his political beliefs and emerged to become the first democratically elected president of South Africa after the end of apartheid. Mandela spent most of his early life fighting against the official South African government's apartheid policy, which severely restricted all the human rights of that country's black population. As founder and leader of the armed wing of the African National Congress, Mandela coordinated sabotage efforts against the government and military. In 1962 he was arrested and eventually charged with using violent means in an attempt to overthrow the government. He spent the next twenty-seven years in prison, much of it at hard labor in a lime quarry on Robben Island. During his time in prison, he earned a Bachelor of Laws degree through a University of London correspondence course. In prison he was treated harshly by the guards; for long periods of time, he was kept apart from the general population and given reduced rations. When his son died, he was not permitted to attend the funeral, and he suffered permanent eye damage because the guards refused to allow him to wear sunglasses in the quarry. But while imprisoned his reputation continued to grow, and he became an inspiration for people all around the world yearning for freedom.

Resentment is like drinking poison
and then hoping it will kill your enemies.
—Nelson Mandela

After being released from prison in 1990, he was asked if he harbored resentment against his captors. He responded, "No, I don't. Resentment is like drinking poison and then hoping it will kill your enemies." He then led the four years of negotiations that ended apartheid in South Africa. When Chris Hani, the leader of the African National Congress party, was assassinated in 1993, the country was on the verge of being torn apart. But at that moment of crisis Mandela addressed the nation, asking for unity: "I am reaching out to every single South African, black and white, from the very depths of my being. A white man, full of prejudice and hate, came to our country and committed a deed so foul that our whole nation now teeters on the brink of disaster. A white woman, of Afrikaner origin, risked her life so that we may know, and bring to justice, this assassin . . . Now is the time for all South Africans to stand together against those who, from any quarter, wish to destroy what Chris Hani gave his life for—the freedom of all of us."

For adhering to the principles of nonviolent leadership, just as Gandhi had earlier done, in 1993 Nelson Mandela was awarded the Nobel Peace Prize. A year later he was elected president, and instead of punishing those people who had committed crimes during apartheid, he set an example that may never be forgotten. He embraced a policy of reconciliation, announcing that those people who would confess to crimes committed during apartheid would be forgiven. In fact, among the invited guests to his inauguration were several of his prison guards.

A respected business consultant and author of the bestselling book *Good to Great,* Jim Collins understands that many great leaders have had this role thrust upon them. They didn't choose it, often it chose them. "The good-to-great leaders never wanted to become larger-than-life heroes. They never aspired to be put on a pedestal or become unreachable icons. They were seemingly ordinary people quietly producing extraordinary results."

Certainly one of Jim Collins's ordinary people

would be Bill W., the founder of Alcoholics Anonymous. By 1934 Bill Wilson's alcoholism threatened to destroy his life. His drinking had prevented him from graduating from law school, destroyed his career on Wall Street, damaged his marriage, and jeopardized his health. He was hospitalized in New York City four times for alcoholism and warned by doctors that if he didn't stop drinking, he would die or be locked up permanently in a detoxification ward. At that time in history it was widely believed that alcoholism was a moral failing or a choice, rather than a medical condition. Wilson desperately wanted to stop drinking, he just couldn't seem to do it. He tried all the known cures of that time, and as each one failed he tried the next one. He was resilient, but he was losing the battle to this terrible disease. During his final stay in the hospital he was given the belladonna cure, a mixture of hallucinogenic drugs, which caused him to have an intense spiritual reaction. In his delirium he suddenly saw a white flash and believed he had been saved. From that moment on he never had another drink. He then set out to help other alcoholics overcome their addictions.

The concept that became AA was born during a trip to Akron, Ohio, when Bill Wilson was tempted to have a drink and reached out for help. He called a local church and was put in touch with a member of an evangelical group, another alcoholic named Dr. Bob Smith. Together Bill Wilson and Dr. Bob Smith discovered that alcoholics could support each other in their efforts to stop drinking. The idea spread slowly, but after more than a hundred alcoholics meeting regularly in church groups in both New York and Akron had become sober, Wilson wrote a book he titled *Alcoholics Anonymous*. Included in that book were twelve steps alcoholics could take on their path to sobriety. Using that book as a model, Alcoholics Anonymous groups were organized around the country. Through the years more than one hundred thousand registered AA groups have helped millions of men and women fight the disease of alcoholism. As author Susan Cheever wrote in her biography of Wilson, *My Name is Bill,* "Wilson never held himself up as a model: he only hoped to help other people by sharing his own experience, strength and hope. He insisted again and again that he was just an ordinary man." An ordinary man whose resiliency transformed millions of lives.

The purpose of life is a life of purpose.

—Robert Byrne

7

SENSE OF PURPOSE

Great leaders possess a sense of purpose. As the American philosopher and humorist Robert Byrne pointed out, "The purpose of life is a life of purpose." Finding that purpose can be difficult and take a great deal of time. As Pastor Rick Warren, the author of bestselling *The Purpose Driven Life,* wrote, "Being successful and fulfilling your life's purpose are not at all the same thing; You can reach all your personal goals, become a raving success by the world's standard—and still miss your purpose in life." But once a leader finds a meaningful reason to follow a path, they will stay that course as long and as far as it takes them. One of those people was a young man named Satish Kumar. He was born in a very small village in Rajastan, India. When he was nine years old he told his mother, a widow, that he wanted to join a wandering sect of monks known as Jains. The Jains live a completely austere, ascetic, nonviolent life in which they harm no living thing, from humans to ants to plants, even rocks and water. When they walk at night they sweep the floor in front of them so as not to step on an ant. Satish Kumar's mother, who had introduced him to the Jains' way of life, was not surprised, "I've been dreading this moment," she told him. "I saw this in a dream." But she gave him permission to join them.

Nine years later, after reading the works of Gandhi, the eighteen-year-old Kumar left the Jain monastery to become a disciple of Vinoba Bhave, whom Indians considered Gandhi's spiritual successor. Bhave followed the precepts of nonviolence, walking around India trying to convince wealthy landowners to give a small part of their property to the country's most destitute and poor, members of the lowest caste known as the Untouchables. He successfully collected five million acres of land. Kumar walked with him for three years until, in 1962, he read a story in an English-language newspaper called the *Daily Herald* reporting that the ninety-year-old Nobel Prize–winning writer and philosopher Lord Bertrand Russell had been arrested and put in prison in London for protesting the nuclear arms race then taking place in the four richest nations in the world. He was so impressed by Russell's civil disobedience that he felt compelled to do something for world peace, and decided he would go to the capitals of the four nuclear nations: Moscow, Paris, London, and Washington, D.C. But if he flew to those places and stayed in hotels, he knew, he would be just like everyone else and no one would pay attention to him. Instead, he would express his protest by walking halfway around the world for peace.

A friend of his named Mannon agreed to go

with him. When Kumar told Bhave about this plan, Bhave gave them his blessing and his two most powerful "gifts" for their protection: "One, go without any money on you. And secondly, you are vegetarian; remain vegetarian." Without money, he explained, they would be forced to find kind people to help them, and, when asked about their vegetarian diet, they would be able to tell people about their peaceful beliefs.

Satish Kumar had found his purpose in life, and, as he discovered, his purpose proved uplifting for so many others. It certainly was a quixotic adventure. While they were walking through the Khyber Pass between Pakistan and Afghanistan, a car stopped and the American driver offered them a ride. When they explained their mission, the driver asked their destination. They explained: "We are walking eventually to the United States of America . . . [We know that] it's beyond many hills, and beyond many countries, and beyond the ocean, and everything. We have seen it on the map. But one day we'll be there." The driver smiled and wished them well on their journey.

When they reached Armenia in the Soviet Union they met two women walking on a road. When they told the women their purpose, one of them suggested, "We work in the tea factory. Why don't you come in and have a cup of tea?" At the tea factory one of the women handed them four tea bags and said they must take them with them. "[T]hese four packets are very, very important," she said. "I would like you to carry one to our Premier, one to the President of France, one to the Prime Minister of England, and one to the President of the United States of America. And I want you to take our message from this factory that if ever they get a mad thought of pushing the nuclear button to please stop for one minute and have a fresh cup of tea from these packets. And then they will have a moment to think and contemplate, and they will realize that the people who are producing tea, working in the factories, working in the fields, working in normal life, leading an ordinary life, are not their enemies. We are ordinary people, and we have done nothing to deserve a nuclear attack."

Kumar and Mannon decided they would deliver these tea bags, and this message, to the leaders of the four countries who possessed nuclear weapons. In Moscow they were greeted by Prime Minister Khrushchev's deputy. In Paris they were arrested for participating in a demonstration supporting a proposed nuclear-test-ban treaty. They were held in a filthy cell for four days, then deported to England, where they handed a tea bag to a representative of Prime Minister Harold Wilson and met Lord Russell, who raised the money that allowed them to sail to New York on the *Queen Mary*. In America they met with Martin Luther King and handed the fourth tea bag to a representative of President Lyndon Johnson. The pilgrimage covered eight thousand miles, and Kumar wrote about his adventures in his book, *Path Without Destination*.

When asked what he had learned on his journey, he explained, "[W]hen people really desire peace, the governments will have to do it . . . [T]he force and the strength for peace will come from people. And that will happen when people start to realize that all the diversity and differences we see of nationalities, of religions, of cultures, of languages, are all beautiful diversities, for they are only on the surface. And deep down we share the same humanity, the global humanity."

For Satish Kumar his walk was only a beginning. He eventually settled in England, where he has edited the magazine *Resurgence* and helped found several schools that focus on ecological issues. At the age of fifty he did a walking pilgrimage to all the sacred places in Britain. And in 2006, American Congressman Dennis Kucinich stood up in the House of Representatives and said, "I rise today in honor and recognition of Satish Kumar, for a lifetime dedicated to teaching and serving as an inspiration to

Follow your bliss and doors will open where there were no doors before.

—Joseph Campbell

all. Mr. Kumar has done more, seen more, accomplished more and walked more than most and has never ceased in bringing his message to others."

Joseph Campbell, who has written so beautifully about mythology, was eloquent when he advised, "Follow your bliss and doors will open where there were no doors before." People like Papa Jaime and Satish Kumar did not set out to change the world, they simply were following their bliss.

It was from my father that I learned the true value of having a sense of purpose. My father was a cardiologist and a professor of medicine. I was seven years old, a very impressionable age, when we moved from Poona to the city of Jabalpur in central India. Although my father was a physician in the Indian army, he was also permitted to maintain a private practice. He established a clinic in our home, and his reputation as an amazing clinician and a caring and compassionate man spread throughout India. People would come from all over the country to be treated by him. He treated everyone who came to our home, whether they arrived in a Mercedes or had walked a great distance to get there, with equal dignity. We knew of many people who traveled hundreds of miles to see Doctor Chopra. My mother would greet each patient and learned to determine what they could afford by asking a few questions. For the poor she would very quietly advise the secretary, "Don't charge these people for this visit and serve them tea and snacks. Give them money sufficient for the return train fare."

We lived in Jabalpur for three years, and then the army sent my father to another post. When we went to the train station to leave at least a thousand people had gathered on the platform to wish the doctor farewell. This was not an organized gathering; they had each come on their own. Many of them were crying because Dr. Chopra, their savior, was leaving them. I was ten years old, and at that moment I decided to become a physician like my father.

The everlasting wisdom of the Brandeis University professor Morrie Schwartz was celebrated by

. . . When people find their purpose in life and pursue it, their leadership is exemplary and authentic and others will be inspired to follow them.

Mitch Albom in his bestselling book *Tuesdays with Morrie* and has served as an inspiration to millions of people around the world. Among the many things that Morrie told Albom when they met each Tuesday afternoon was, "The way you get meaning into your life is to devote yourself to loving others, devote yourself to the community around you and devote yourself to something that gives you purpose and meaning." And as I have seen, when people find their purpose in life and pursue it, their leadership is exemplary and authentic and others will be inspired to follow them.

8

HUMILITY

Great leaders are humble—and they have a sense of humor. They have the ability to keep their achievements, and their ego, in perspective. Sir Edmund Hillary, who made history and became world-famous in 1953 when he became the first man to reach the summit of Mount Everest, said, "I was just an enthusiastic mountaineer of modest abilities who was willing to work quite hard and had the necessary imagination and determination. I was just an average bloke. It was the media that transformed me into this heroic figure and try as I did there was no way to destroy my heroic image. But as I learned through the years, as long as you don't believe all that rubbish about yourself you won't come to much harm."

Before Hillary's success, seven major expeditions had failed in their attempts to reach the highest point in the world. Hillary and his Sherpa guide, Tenzing Norgay, were the only members of his large expedition to accomplish that feat—and Hillary only survived when Norgay saved his life on the mountain. There was little reason to expect Hillary would succeed where so many others had failed; he lived in New Zealand and was a beekeeper. There was nothing extraordinary about him—until he stood on the top of the world. Ironically, it was not climbing the mountain but rather what he did after coming down from the mountain that gave Hillary the most satisfaction. In the years that followed, he created the Himalayan Trust for the people of Nepal, building more than sixty-three schools, two hospitals, medical clinics, bridges, and even airfields. The trust also rebuilt monasteries and improved the local roads. It was on the way to the dedication of one of

When asked if he believed conquering Mount Everest was the greatest accomplishment of his life, Sir Edmund Hillary responded, "No, all I did was leave a footprint on the mountain. My greatest contribution has been the building of schools and medical clinics for the poor people of Nepal.

those schools that Hillary suffered the worst tragedy of his life when his wife and his teenage daughter died in a plane crash. But rather than withdrawing from his work, he increased his efforts to answer the needs of the Nepalese. When asked if he believed conquering Mount Everest was the greatest accomplishment of his life, Sir Edmund Hillary responded, "No, all I did was leave a footprint on the mountain. My greatest contribution has been the building of schools and medical clinics for the poor people of Nepal."

Asked once why he had climbed the mountain, he explained, "I've always felt that it's far more important to set your sights high. Aim for something high, and even fail on it if necessary." Although, of course, in his particular case there was nothing higher in the world at which to aim.

The philosopher, physician, and theologist Albert Schweitzer was awarded the Nobel Peace Prize in 1952 for his philosophy, which he described as reverence for life, and also for founding a hospital in

Africa in which he treated patients for decades. Upon receiving that honor—and using the money awarded to build a leper colony at his hospital— he graciously thanked the committee and then said, with great humility, "They gave me the Peace Prize—I don't know why. Now I feel I should do something to earn it!"

Fareed Zakaria hosts a weekly show on CNN known as *GPS,* meaning "global public square," on which he focuses on international issues. One Sunday morning he had as his guest Bill Gates, the cofounder of Microsoft and one of the wealthiest men in the world who has chosen to give away billions of dollars through his foundation. At the end of the interview Zakaria asked him, "Do you think history will re- member you as the man who created Microsoft, or the man who created the Gates Foundation?"

Gates smiled, then said, "Who knows how his- tory will think of me? You know, the person who played bridge with Warren Buffett, maybe. Or maybe not at all."

If I have seen further than others,
it is because I have stood on the
shoulders of Giants.

—*Sir Isaac Newton*

Ted Turner, the founder of CNN, and like Gates a notable philanthropist, once said facetiously, "If I only had a little humility, I would be perfect."

Sir Isaac Newton, who built the first practical telescope and whose description of the laws of gravity and motion transformed our understanding of the universe, engaged in a long rivalry with Robert Hooke, the first curator of the Royal Society, an organization of notable scientists formed in about 1645 that created a uniform structure by which experiments would be conducted. In response to a letter from Hooke challenging his originality, Newton wrote, "If I have seen further than others, it is because I have stood on the shoulders of Giants."

It is the quality of humility that often enables leaders to break down the barriers between themselves and those who follow, and that makes them worthy of esteem. Among the many traits that made Abraham Lincoln so beloved was his humility. There was a well-known story that during the Civil War a servant went into the basement of the White

House and, to his astonishment, found the president sitting on a bench, hard at work shining his boots. "Mr. President," he exclaimed, "what are you doing? Why are you shining your own boots?" Lincoln paused, looked at the man, and asked, "What do you mean? Whose boots should I be shining?"

For me, just as I learned the importance of a sense of purpose from my father, it was my mother who taught our family grace and humility. As most people are aware, there is both great wealth and great poverty in India, and throughout history a strictly enforced caste system existed. While my parents were successful people, in everything they did they reminded my brother and me that all human beings are deserving of equal respect. This was brought home to me, literally, one night when my parents' dinner was interrupted by three young men. They burst into our house wearing masks and carrying guns. They beat the servant who worked for us and tied up my mother and father, demanding from them all the fees from the clinic. My mother was a very docile lady, but in this instance she spoke loudly. "You obviously have needs," she said. "And we will take care of them. I'll give you more than the fees, but stop beating this young man. He has a family and he's innocent. If you want to kill, kill my husband and me." And then she added, "Our sons are settled in America. We've lived a full life."

The thieves were so astonished they ceased attacking the servant. In addition to the cash in the clinic, my mother gave them the jewelry she was wearing, including her earrings. My mother never believed that material wealth made one person more important than others. When the robbers started to leave, their leader paused and came over to her. "I'm sorry I'm doing this," he said. "I need to do it." He then handed back her earrings, "Please put these back on your ears. You have amazing grace and courage, and your face looks bare without them." Then he touched her feet and asked for her blessing.

My mother told him, "God be with you. I will pray that you mend your ways."

Like humility, humor is an effective means through which leaders connect with people. It may be the best tool of all to puncture the balloons of pomposity. The rivalry between British Prime Ministers Benjamin Disraeli and William Gladstone was well known, and the two men disliked each other intensely. One day in Parliament Disraeli made a comment about misfortune, and the next day a reporter approached him and asked, "Prime Minister, in your mind what's the difference between misfortune and calamity?"

Disraeli paused only briefly before explaining, "If Gladstone fell into the Thames, that would be a misfortune. But if someone were to drag him out, that would be a calamity."

Perhaps more than any of the founding fathers, Benjamin Franklin had a wonderful sense of humor. Even in his dotage, with a twinkle in his eye he delighted in telling a group of women, "If you ladies have any questions—the answer is yes!" In his lifetime Franklin became almost as famous for his witticisms as he had become for his inventions and contributions to freedom. His sayings were widely quoted through the nation. And on the subject of humility, he understood, "He that falls in love with himself will have no rivals."

In 1981 President Ronald Reagan was shot during an assassination attempt. In fact, because he was able to walk and speak after the shooting few people realized his life was in jeopardy. He was rushed to George Washington Hospital in Washington, D.C. When Nancy Reagan arrived, Reagan's first words to her were, "Honey, I forgot to duck." And as he was wheeled into the operating room for emergency surgery, he was able to put the medical team that was about to try to save the life of the most powerful man in the world at ease by joking, "Please tell me you're all Republicans."

A Gallup/CNN/USA TODAY poll conducted in 1999 found that the evangelist Billy Graham was America's seventh most admired person of the twentieth century. Graham, who claims to have preached to more people than any minister in history, certainly understood the importance of humor in reaching listeners. His sermons were often sprinkled with humor; for example, he once admitted to his followers, "The only time my prayers are never answered is on the golf course."

Few American presidents were more popular while in office than John Kennedy, and part of the reason for that was his celebrated sense of humor. Just after being elected, for example, he was accused by Republicans of buying his victory. In response, he said, "I've just received the following wire from my generous Daddy, 'Dear Jack. Don't buy a single vote more than is necessary. I'll be damned if I'm going to pay for a landslide!'"

In 1930 Gandhi visited England to bring attention to the brutal tactics being used by the British army to quell the growing freedom movement in India. Thousands of Indians had been beaten and imprisoned for protesting, so when a reporter asked

Gandhi, "What do you think of western civilization?" He replied, "I think it would be a good idea."

Israeli Prime Minister Golda Meir was legendary for her ability to find the humor in difficult situations. As she once pointed out, even Moses made mistakes. "He dragged us for 40 years through the desert to bring us to the one place in the Middle East where there was no oil." And finally, she could also be as tough and blunt as any male politician. As she once advised General Moshe Dayan, "Don't be so humble. You're not that great."

Great leaders have integrity as well

as great ideas.

Imagine your integrity to be a bright balloon. It can last almost forever, until it gets just the slightest prick—and then it is burst and gone, never to be whole again.

9

INTEGRITY

Great leaders have integrity as well as great ideas. The Bard, William Shakespeare, considered integrity far more valuable than money, writing in *Othello,* "Good name in man and woman, dear my lord, is the immediate jewel of their souls. Who steals my purse steals trash; 'tis something, nothing; 'Twas mine, 'tis his, and has been slave to thousands; But he that filches from me my good name, robs me of that which not enriches him, and makes me poor indeed."

Integrity in a leader is the consistent pattern of upholding a high standard of moral and ethical behavior. As a Chinese proverb tells us, "If you stand straight, do not fear a crooked shadow." Which, I suppose, was expressed in a more straightforward manner by the American frontiersman Davy Crockett, who later died defending the Alamo but stood by his philosophy, "Be sure you're right—then go ahead!"

Imagine your integrity to be a bright balloon. It can last almost forever, until it gets just the slightest prick—and then it is burst and gone, never to be whole again. The fact is that you can do something perfectly for thirty years or even a lifetime. Then, if you do one thing to compromise your integrity, you have sullied your reputation forever. As the investor Warren Buffett pointed out, "It takes twenty years to build a reputation and five minutes to ruin it." The Greek philosopher Heraclitus said to the ages, "The soul is dyed the color of its thoughts; think only those things that are in line with your principles and can bear the full light of day. The content of your character is your choice. Day by day what you choose, what you think and what you do is who you become. Your integrity is your destiny."

Few leaders have ever demonstrated their integrity at greater cost than Sir Thomas More, whom King Henry VIII appointed the Lord Chancellor of England in 1529. But when the king demanded that his marriage to Catherine be annulled so he could marry Anne Boleyn within the Church, More refused to recognize the marriage. What happened then has become legend and has been celebrated in literature and film for centuries, most familiarly in the play and movie *A Man for All Seasons*. When More refused to take an oath that would have acknowledged the legitimacy of the king's marriage, Henry had him imprisoned in the Tower of London. He was tortured and all his property was taken. To be free and have his life and property restored, all More had to do was take the oath that recognized Henry as the new head of the Catholic Church in England. In the play, written by Robert Bolt, More explains, "When a man takes an oath . . . he's holding his own self in his hands. Like water. And if he opens his fingers then—he needn't hope to find himself again."

For his refusal to take the oath, Thomas More was found guilty of treason and beheaded.

There is a story told about General Dwight Eisenhower that illustrates the meaning of integrity. As the commander of the Allied Expeditionary Force in World War II it was his task to launch the greatest invasion force in history. 160,000 troops in more than 5,000 ships awaited his order to attack the heavily fortified shores of France. If he made the wrong decision, if he picked the wrong moment, the invasion might fail and Hitler would remain in control of Europe. The weather forecast for early June 1944 was poor, but there appeared to be a window of good weather on the sixth. With the fate of the free world at stake, Eisenhower didn't hesitate; he gave the order to launch the invasion. The success propelled him to the presidency of the United States. And when asked about making that historic deci-

Small minds discuss people,
average minds discuss events,
great minds discuss ideas.

—Eleanor Roosevelt

sion, he said, "The supreme quality for leadership is unquestionably integrity. Without it, no real success is possible, no matter whether it is on a section gang, a football field, in an army, or in an office."

Great leaders have great ideas. The first lady of the United States, Eleanor Roosevelt, was fiercely independent, even disagreeing publicly with the policies of her husband, President Franklin Roosevelt. She published six books and wrote scores of articles and was an ardent advocate for civil rights. She once famously declared, "Small minds discuss people, average minds discuss events, great minds discuss ideas."

She was admired far and wide. She died at age seventy-eight in 1962. At her memorial service, Adlai Stevenson asked, "What other single human being has touched and transformed the existence of so many?" and reminded the world that she was "someone who would rather light a candle than curse the darkness."

Albert Einstein, whose theory of relativity changed

the way scientists understand the workings of the universe, believed that "The true sign of intelligence is not knowledge, but imagination. Imagination is more important than knowledge. Knowledge is limited, imagination encircles the world." Einstein actually began developing his theory of relativity when he was sixteen years old and first imagined what it might be like to ride through the universe alongside a ray of light.

It is imagination that allows great leaders to embrace change. They see failure in holding on to the status quo and forge new paths. As the poet Ralph Waldo Emerson once wrote, "Do not go where the path may lead; go instead where there is no path and leave a trail."

Imagination is the engine of invention. A single idea can change the world. David Packard and William Hewlett began with $538, making simple electronic devices in Packard's garage as varied as electronic harmonica tuning instruments, exercise machines, and a foul-line alarm for bowling lanes.

Do not go where the path may lead;

go instead where there is no path

and leave a trail.

—Ralph Waldo Emerson

Eventually they began producing electronic measuring devices, and Hewlett-Packard became one of the largest information-technology companies in the world. Packard ignored traditional business models while building HP, encouraging the creativity that led to many revolutionary products through an innovative open-door policy. He literally designed executive offices without doors and put his employees in open cubicles to facilitate communication. As he wrote, "The driving force for the development of new products is not technology, not money, but the imagination of people."

Few leaders have shown more imagination throughout their careers than Lee Iacocca. Trained as an engineer, Iacocca instead worked in sales at Ford. He first gained attention by creating the $56 in '56 campaign, which allowed people to buy a 1956 Ford for $56 a month. Several years later, he created the Ford Mustang, an affordable, sporty car with a powerful image that became one of the most successful car models in history. When he took over

The only limit to your impact
is your imagination.

—Tony Robbins, bestselling self-help author

the failing Chrysler Corporation in 1978, many business leaders believed the company could not be saved. In response, Iacocca said optimistically, "A wise man will make more opportunities than he finds." In the next few years he introduced several new models, streamlined that company, and turned it into a great American success story.

The bestselling self-help author and success coach Tony Robbins perhaps summed up the importance of imagination best when he said, "The only limit to your impact is your imagination."

Leaders appreciate the fact that the people in their organizations are the most valuable assets.

10

PACKING OTHERS'
PARACHUTES

The final letter in the leadership mnemonic stands for three attributes: people skills, principles, and packing others' parachutes. Great leaders have people skills; they adhere strongly to their principles, and they pack other people's parachutes. Few structures in history have been considered more impregnable than the Great Wall of China, which was built to protect China's northern border from invading nomads. The Great Wall actually was built in many sections over centuries, and those pieces were eventually connected to make a structure almost 4,000 miles long, at an average height of 25 feet, and between 15- and 30-feet wide. Yet China's enemies still managed to successfully invade the country twice. How did they do it? Did they invent some military weapon great enough to knock holes in the wall? Did they scale it at night, perhaps with magical ropes and ladders? No, of course not. The armies of the Ming Dynasty successfully held off the invading Manchus for almost half a century—until a general who was bitter at the way he was being treated simply opened the gates for them.

Leaders appreciate the fact that the people in their organizations are the most valuable assets. And the way you deal with them on a regular basis defines those relationships. Indira Gandhi, who served as India's prime minister four times, understood that, as she explained, "I suppose leadership at one time meant muscles; but today it means getting along with people." She noted memorably, "You cannot shake hands with a clenched fist."

The industrialist Andrew Carnegie was one of America's wealthiest men—and he gave away most of his fortune to community causes. Carnegie understood that his success was due to so many other people, pointing out, "No man will ever make a great leader who wants to do it all by himself or to get all the credit for doing it."

And I wonder if there has ever been a better definition of leadership than that expressed by British Prime Minister Benjamin Disraeli, who said simply, "I must follow the people. Am I not their leader?"

In 2008, I had the privilege of meeting a man named Charlie Plumb, a retired United States Navy Captain, when I invited him to serve as a keynote speaker at a week-long Harvard Medical School postgraduate course, Update in Internal Medicine. And he told me his story. Charlie Plumb flew a Phantom jet on seventy-four successful missions in Vietnam. But in May 1967, on his seventy-fifth and final mission, five days before he was scheduled to return home, he was shot down. He was twenty-four years old and had married his high school sweetheart at the chapel at the Naval Academy three years earlier. He was captured by villagers who put him in a pen with a bull, giving him, as he later wrote, "his first opportunity to play matador."

Eventually he was put into an 8×8 foot cell. Because he refused to cooperate with his captors he was tortured and kept isolated for months. But one day he heard what sounded like a cricket chirping in a corner of his filthy cell. He discovered it wasn't a cricket but that the scratching sound was being made by a slender piece of wire poking out of a hole in the wall. When he tugged at it, it disappeared into the wall. After some time it reappeared with a slip of toilet paper attached to the end. It was a message from a fellow prisoner. "I've been here for two years," it read. "Memorize this code and swallow this paper." Utilizing this basic tap code—tap, pause, tap for the letter "a"; tap, pause, two taps for "b"; and so on—he finally was able to communicate with the

other men in the prison. Through the wire and oc-
casional conversations in the mess, Charlie Plumb
was able to eventually become a leader.

As he learned, there were 191 prisoners of war in
this camp, all of them American fighter-jet pilots
with the exception of a nineteen-year-old sailor who
had fallen off an aircraft carrier while asleep. Inside
the prison the others made fun of this sailor, telling
him that this was an elite prisoner-of-war camp and
that he didn't belong there. After this sailor spent
two years in the camp, the Viet Cong agreed to release him. Initially the sailor refused to go, insisting
he was a member of the team and that he wouldn't
desert his fellow prisoners. All of us or none of us,
he told them. But Plumb practically ordered him
to go, telling him, "I'm Commander of this camp,
you take that release and go." The reasoning was
simple: that sailor had memorized the names, social
security numbers, and telephone numbers of every
prisoner in the camp. After he was released he criss-
crossed America, north to south, east to west, visiting

the homes of as many prisoners as possible, telling their family, your husband is alive, your father is alive, and passing along as much information as possible.

Charlie Plumb spent almost six years in prison. From the group emerged three admirals, two congressman, and one senator who almost became the president of the United States, John McCain. Charlie Plumb has become one of the country's most respected motivational speakers and has told his story of courage and perseverance to more than 4,500 audiences. And he also tells the story of what happened to him many years after his release: he was sitting in a diner with his wife having breakfast and a man sitting nearby kept staring at him. Finally, the man walked over and asked, "Excuse me, but are you Charlie Plumb?" Plumb nodded. "You were flying off the *Kitty Hawk,* your plane was shot down, you ejected and were captured and spent six years as a prisoner of war and you were tortured?"

Captain Plumb looked right at him and said, "That's all true, but who are you?"

The man smiled. "I'm the guy who packed your parachute. Obviously, it worked."

The point Captain Plumb is making is that leadership isn't a one-way street; at some point every leader will have to depend on other people, just as those other people will depend on them. When I heard this story I realized I had never thanked the people who packed my parachute. In my professional career there were four or five people who gave me the support that made all the difference, and I realized I had never expressed my appreciation. So I sat down and sent a note to Dr. Eugene Braunwald, chairman and physician-in-chief of the Department of Medicine at Brigham and Women's Hospital in Boston. Dr. Braunwald was my mentor. He nurtured my career in so many ways. I told him how instrumental he had been in furthering my career and then added that I have often referred to him as 'God in medicine,' and that he had, indeed, packed my parachute.

I then wrote similar letters to four other mentors

of mine. Expressing genuine gratitude was absolutely thrilling and fulfilling for me.

Most of us have been fortunate in that someone packed our parachute. It may have been a parent or a teacher or a friend. I urge you not to wait for the eulogy; express your gratitude now, and it will be immensely gratifying to all. Then, as a leader, go back and pack other people's parachutes.

Dr. Ben Carson is one of the most inspiring people I have had the pleasure of knowing. In fact, he has served as the keynote speaker at seven annual conferences called Current Clinical Issues in Primary Care that I am privileged to direct and speak at around the country. Dr. Carson grew up in the depths of poverty in Detroit. His mother had dropped out of school in third grade and had been married at thirteen. Her husband abandoned her when she discovered he was a bigamist. As a fifth grader Ben was at the bottom of his class, the other children teased him and called him "dummy," and he had a violent temper. It would have been easy to predict that he was doomed to fall into the familiar pattern of poverty and failure, and, with his temper, probably end up in prison. But that's not what happened. Instead, Ben graduated from Yale and the University of Michigan Medical School. He became a respected neurosurgeon and, at thirty-two years old, was the youngest full professor in the history of world-renowned Johns Hopkins Hospital, where he was the Director of Pediatric Neurosurgery. In 2008, for his work saving the lives of young people, Carson was awarded the Presidential Medal of Freedom, the highest government award that can be given to a civilian.

How was that possible? How could Ben Carson rise from that difficult childhood to become such a nationally respected physician? Somebody cared. Somebody cared enough to make a difference. In his case it was his mother. When asked who was the greatest inspiration in his life, who had packed his parachute, he has always replied it was his mother. As he explained, she refused to go on welfare and

Great leaders also adhere to their principles. Principles are the moral compass by which you sail your own ship.

instead worked as a domestic servant; at times, when it was necessary, she worked two jobs. She limited the time Ben and his siblings were permitted to watch television to about two hours each week. She also did one other remarkable thing: she made them read two library books a week and write book reports for her. Dr. Carson said to me, "It wasn't until I left for college that I realized my mother did not know how to read. She would get a neighbor to grade the papers for her."

Great leaders also adhere to their principles. A principle is simply a belief or set of beliefs by which you lead your life. Principles are the moral compass by which you sail your own ship. As Shakespeare wrote in *Hamlet,* "To thine own self be true, and it must follow, as the night the day, thou canst not then be false to any man." There is the apocryphal story of the shopkeeper who noticed that as a woman customer left his store a $20 bill had dropped out of her pocket. As the door closed behind her this shopkeeper picked up the money and hesitated. This was the kind of moment that tested his principles. No one knew about the money except him. He realized he was faced with a terribly difficult moral dilemma: should he keep the money himself or share it with his partner?

The legendary radio and television journalist Edward R. Murrow risked his career in 1954 when he used his television program *See It Now* to launch an attack on powerful Senator Joseph McCarthy. Without producing evidence, McCarthy had claimed that there were Communists working in the government, the military, and the media and that he knew who they were. In this climate of fear, those named by McCarthy and the people with whom he was allied were blacklisted. Being blacklisted destroyed lives and careers. Murrow was a firm believer in American civil liberties, including the constitutional safeguards of free speech. On his program he risked destroying his own career to defend the principles in which he believed, reminding his viewers, "The line between investigating and persecuting is a very fine one and the junior senator from Wisconsin has stepped over it repeatedly . . . We must remember always that accusation is not proof and that conviction depends upon evidence and due process of law. We will not walk in fear, one of another. We will not be driven by fear into an age of unreason."

But he went much further than that. One of those people blacklisted was a popular radio personality named John Henry Faulk. Faulk had lost his job, and, without an income, he was about to lose his house. When Murrow heard about that, he gave Faulk the $2,000 needed to save it. At first Faulk refused to take the money, telling Murrow, "I can't take this. I don't know if I can ever pay you back."

But Murrow insisted, telling Faulk, "This isn't a loan. It's an investment in America." For Murrow, defending the principles in which he believed was worth much more than $2,000.

In 1981 the Indian computer engineer N. R. Narayana Murthy and six friends borrowed $250 from

Leaders with principle are less likely to get bullied and pushed around because they can draw clear lines in the sand. The softest pillow is a clear conscience.

—N. R. Narayana Murthy

his wife, Sudha, who actually pawned a piece of jewelry to raise the money, and used it to found Infosys, an information technology company in Bangalore, India. Setting up his first office, Murthy wanted a telephone installed in his office. That sounds simple enough, but at that time in India the telephone system was controlled by bureaucrats who demanded an additional payment, a bribe, to move him ahead on the long waiting list. He refused—on principle. He was adamant that he was not going to start his company by paying a bribe. Finally, after waiting a year, the telephone was installed. And after a rough beginning Infosys has become one of the largest IT companies in the world, employing almost 115,000 people in thirty-three countries and generating annual revenues of more than $60 billion—and accomplishing that while adhering to Narayana Murthy's principles. In 2005 *The Economist* named Murthy the seventh most admired CEO in the world on a list that included Warren Buffett, Bill Gates, and Steve Jobs. "A true leader," he once said, "is one who leads by example and sacrifices more than anyone else, in his or her pursuit of excellence . . . Leaders with principle are less likely to get bullied and pushed around because they can draw clear lines in the sand. The softest pillow is a clear conscience."

For great leaders, principle is far more important than personal gain. Norman Borlaug grew up on a farm in Iowa, and, like many young farmers, wondered why plants grew better in some areas than others. After earning a doctorate in plant pathology from the University of Minnesota, he began working as a microbiologist at DuPont. In 1944, when he was offered a job with the Rockefeller Foundation's Hunger Project in Mexico, DuPont offered to double his salary if he would stay with that company. Although he was married and the father of a baby, and certainly that increased salary would have eased his life, he turned down DuPont's offer and instead moved to Mexico. When he arrived he discovered that Mexican farmers had overfarmed their land, depriving the soil of vital nutrients. The crops were diseased and the yields per acre were so low that farmers could barely feed their own families. "I don't know what we can do to help these people," he wrote to his wife, "but we've got to do something." This was the beginning of the "green revolution." Working in Mexican fields and laboratories, he discovered that by genetically altering wheat plants, production on the same acreage could be tripled and quadrupled, a discovery that later was applied to improving rice yields in Asia. His discoveries eventually allowed Mexican farmers to increase their wheat production sixfold and subsequently were applied to agriculture around the world, from Chile to China. For example, in three decades India more than tripled its output of wheat, enabling a country that throughout its history has been faced with food shortages to feed more than two hundred million additional citizens

In 1970, in awarding him the Peace Prize, the Nobel committee wrote, "More than any other single person of this age, he has helped provide bread for a hungry world." As the world population grew, Borlaug's discoveries helped prevent famine, and it has been estimated that his work was instrumental in saving as many as a billion lives.

Often when people hear or read about men like Borlaug or Narayana Murthy, they note that these men and women had more education than they do or had different opportunities—maybe they were older or wealthier or had people supporting them. Many of us fail to think of ourselves as potential leaders. This is especially true of young people. They wonder, what can I do that might make a difference? In fact, age should never be a deterrent to taking a chance that might change lives. It's quite possible that a young man named Justin Zaghi once thought he was too young and inexperienced to make an impact on the world. In 2008 Justin was a student at UCLA when he noticed a poster hanging in a hallway. The message was simple: "Join Project Nicaragua, Help Improve Healthcare." For Justin, this was an opportunity to improve his Spanish-language skills while helping poverty-stricken people. Project Nicaragua had been established in December 2005, when six UCLA undergraduate and medical students volunteered at their own expense to work for ten days at Managua's primary neurosurgical hospital, Hospital Lenin Fonseca. The hospital was poorly equipped, so they brought with them everything from neurosurgical instruments to soap and diapers. Zaghi remembers being inspired by the staff there, who often worked twelve-hour days, slept on the floors, and provided the best possible care with the barest medical essentials.

Among the medical conditions the students encountered there was an unusually high incidence of spina bifida, a life-threatening birth defect. With another student, Zaghi began his own investigation into the cause. From data collected by a local pediatrician, they discovered that the primary cause of this defect was a deficiency of folic acid in pregnant women, a problem that could be solved cheaply and effectively by fortifying rice—a staple of the local diet—with folic acid. Zaghi became a strong advocate of fortifying rice, and eventually the Nicaraguan Ministry of Health passed a law mandating the fortification of rice with folic acid. That legislation is estimated to prevent as many as three thousand cases of spina bifida annually at a minimal cost.

A similar story concerning a young person who saw a problem and decided to fix it took place a lot closer to home. While working a summer job between her freshman and sophomore years at Yale in 2000, in a Danbury, Connecticut, eye doctor's office, nineteen-year-old Jennifer Staple was stunned and saddened to discover how many poor patients were suffering from glaucoma, an easily treatable eye disease that, if unattended, can lead to blindness. Most of these people had never before been examined by an eye doctor and knew nothing about the disease. Returning to school at the end of the summer, she recruited other students and trained them to conduct basic acuity screenings. Then she offered their services to community centers, soup kitchens, libraries, and schools. To facilitate follow-up treatment, she identified free programs that offered eye care for people who couldn't afford it. After graduating in 2003, she was admitted to Stanford Medical School—but deferred admission to expand her program. Within two months, students at twenty-five universities had volunteered and were being trained to help people find eye doctors who could provide the care that was needed. Unite for Sight, as Staple named her program, grew so rapidly that she had to postpone medical school a second year.

The program eventually expanded internationally and, by the end of 2011, had trained more than 8,200 volunteers to help eliminate barriers to care and to support local eye doctors in their examinations of more than 1,300,000 patients. In addition, Unite for Sight had arranged about fifty thousand sight-restoring cataract surgeries in Latin America, Asia, and Africa.

For her work, in 2009 Jennifer Staple received

the American Institute of Public Service's National Jefferson Award for Public Service, the "Nobel Prize" for public service. Once Jennifer wanted to become an ophthalmologist so she might help patients keep or restore their sight. Instead, her own vision allowed her to found an organization, which she now helps run, dedicated to helping those people around the world who most need help.

Obviously age is never a bar to leadership. In 1990 twenty-one-year-old Wendy Kopp was a senior at Princeton when, for her senior thesis, she proposed the creation of a national teaching corps, much like the Peace Corps, that would enlist America's brightest recent college graduates and professionals to teach for two years in low-income communities. Her objective was to recruit the leaders of the future, who would never forget their teaching experience and later in life might continue to find ways to contribute to education. Her professor responded, "My dear Ms. Kopp, you are quite evidently deranged."

But she persisted, going forward to create Teach for America even before she had raised the money to support the organization. Within a year Kopp successfully raised $2.5 million in start-up funding and began recruiting young people who wanted to have a meaningful social impact. In 1990 five hundred young men and women were placed in six communities with underperforming schools. For the 2010–2011 school year the organization received more than 18,000 applications and its 9,000 members were teaching about 400,000 students. And perhaps equally important, 14,000 alumni were moving into leadership positions in business, politics—and education.

What is it that enables people like Justin Zaghi, Jennifer Staple, and Wendy Kopp to recognize a need and find a creative way of responding to it? Harvard Business School Professor of Management Practice Bill George is the author of a wonderful book titled *True North,* for which he interviewed 125 top corporate executives. Professor George writes,

Women have a finely tuned intuitive sense; a keen imagination, patience, empathy, a desire to nurture children, kin and community, a talent for making egalitarian connections with others.

—Helen Fisher

"Just as a compass points towards a magnetic pole, your True North pulls you towards the purpose of your leadership. When you follow your internal compass your leadership will be authentic. Although others may guide or influence you, your truth is derived from your life story and only you can determine what that story should be."

When I think about people like Melissa Poe, Jennifer Staple, and Wendy Kopp, I am reminded how leadership is gender-neutral. Women have served and are serving as exemplary leaders. Helen Fisher, an anthropologist and author has written a wonderful book called *The First Sex: The Natural Talents of Women and How They are Changing the World*. In it she points out, "Women have a finely tuned intuitive sense; a keen imagination, patience, empathy, a desire to nurture children, kin and community, a talent for making egalitarian connections with others."

We need more women on major corporate boards in America. Norway passed a law mandating that major corporations in the country need to have at least 40 percent representation by women.

The error that many of us make when reading these stories about leadership is assuming that these people had different qualities than we have. Maybe we assume they have natural charisma, the quality that attracts other people and makes those people want to follow them. The truth is you don't need charisma to be a leader. I'm reminded of the wonderful story told by a woman who dined on consecutive nights with those British political rivals, William Gladstone and Benjamin Disraeli. Asked what impression the men left, she explained, "When I left the dining room after sitting next to Mr. Gladstone, I thought he was the cleverest man in England. But after sitting next to Mr. Disraeli, I thought I was the cleverest woman in England!"

Are leaders born or made? I am asked that question often and I reply there is a simple answer: both. "Leadership is not about who you are or where you come from. It is about what you do," wrote James

Let's get something straight. Leadership is not preordained. It is not a gene, and it is not a trait. There is no hard evidence to support the assertion that leadership is imprinted in the DNA of only some individuals and that the rest of us missed out and are doomed to be clueless.

—James Kouzes and Barry Posner, The Truth About Leadership

Kouzes and Barry Posner in their book *The Truth About Leadership*. And they continued:

> Our answer? We've never met a leader who wasn't born! We've also never met an accountant, artist, athlete, engineer, lawyer, physician, writer, or zoologist who wasn't born. We're all born. That's a given. It's what you do with what you have before you die that makes the difference.

> Let's get something straight. Leadership is not preordained. It is not a gene, and it is not a trait. There is no hard evidence to support the assertion that leadership is imprinted in the DNA of only some individuals and that the rest of us missed out and are doomed to be clueless.

Leaders often emerge from a crisis. Whether born or made, they rise to meet the situation. The world has seen few better examples of that than we witnessed during the 2010 Chilean mining collapse. When fifty-four-year old Chilean miner Luis Urzua went to work as a shift leader one day in August, he had no reason to expect disaster. Suddenly, his thirty-three-man crew working two thousand feet below ground was trapped by a cave-in. While on the surface the government was warning that there probably would be no survivors, below the earth Urzua took control of a desperate situation. Refusing to allow his men to panic, as soon as the dust in the mine had settled Urzua took three men and explored the tunnel. When he realized they would be trapped for a long time, he immediately imposed strong discipline, establishing a set of rigid rules that gave his men the best chance for survival.

Napoleon once said, "A leader is a dealer in hope," and while these miners waited seventeen days in that hole for any signal from the surface, it was Urzua who provided that hope. He rationed the little food they had—each man received two spoonfuls of tuna and half a glass of milk every forty-eight hours—and insisted that all meals were to be eaten as a group to encourage a feeling of unity. Each man was given assigned tasks and worked a regular twelve-hour shift. Working, sleeping, and sanitary areas were designated to create a sense of normalcy. Using light from the miners' lamps, he simulated day and night and insisted on maintaining a schedule. And when contact with the surface was established, his first words, spoken calmly and firmly, were "shift fore-man speaking."

It would be another fifty-two days before a worldwide effort enabled rescuers to save the min-ers. During those long days, Urzua established order, maintained discipline, and reinforced teamwork. When the miners were finally lifted to safety, they asked one thing: that all of them remain on the site until the last man, Luis Urzua, reached the surface. Under extraordinary conditions, he had become a great leader.

Whether born or made, a common thread among leaders is that they take actions for the greater good.

When they must make a difficult decision, they simply do the right thing. The pharmaceutical industry has been much maligned in recent years as critics claim companies have put profit before people. In some cases that may be true, but the fact is that there are some amazing leaders in that industry, among them Dr. Roy Vagelos. In 1975 a scientist working in the laboratories at Merck discovered that a new drug, found in a scoop of soil dug out of a golf course near Ito, Japan, protected cattle, swine, horses, and other animals against a wide range of parasites, including heartworm. That drug, Ivermectin, eventually proved popular and profitable. Three years later, this same scientist found that a version of that drug, named Mectizan, might also prevent onchocerciasis, or river blindness, a terrible disease that affected tens of millions of people in third-world countries. The drug had the potential to eradicate the disease forever, but the problem was that the people who needed the drug couldn't possibly afford to pay for it. Obviously, some companies would have dropped it right there. But Dr. Vagelos, then running Merck's lab, had to decide whether to shelve this drug that might change the lives of a hundred million people or invest the money it would take to develop and test it. He made the decision to go ahead. Almost a decade later, after it had been proved that this drug, Mectizan, could prevent this disease, Vagelos tried to convince our government as well as foundations and charities to sponsor the manufacture and distribution. When it became obvious no one was going to pay those costs, Vagelos, who by that time had become Merck's CEO, made another astonishing decision—Merck would simply give it away. "I had no choice," he later explained. "[W]e had a drug sitting on the shelf that was going to prevent eighteen, twenty, fifty million people from becoming blind. And we stepped up to it and said that we would contribute it free to anyone in the world for as long as it was re-quired."

While some stockholders objected, Vagelos never

wavered. As he said, "My whole life has been dedicated to helping people and this was it for me. What's the cost of preventing 18 million people from going blind?"

Merck has now been producing this drug for more than two decades. It is estimated that more than forty million people in thirty-four countries have received the drug, which has to be taken once a year to effectively prevent the disease. It's impossible to determine how many millions of people retained their sight because of Vagelos's controversial decision. But as *The New York Times* wrote, "Merck's development of Mectizan will surely rank as one of the century's great medical triumphs." And for seven consecutive years *Fortune* 500 leaders voted Merck America's most admired company. Outside the Geneva headquarters of the World Health Organization there is a seven-foot-high statue of an old person who has gone blind from river blindness being led by his sighted grandson, who would have otherwise lost his sight if Roy Vagelos and Merck hadn't made the expensive and courageous commitment to do the right thing. A similar statue was erected outside Merck's headquarters in the United States. It is called *The Gift of Sight*. Both these statues are in tribute to Roy Vagelos's leadership. It has helped formulate the concept of pharmacophilanthropy, something that is now being espoused by other pharmaceutical companies.

Years later Vagelos was asked about the impact his decision made at Merck. "When we approved it, morale at Merck skyrocketed . . . The people of Merck were absolutely ecstatic. They said, 'You know we never thought we would ever do something this good.' And it assured Merck's being able to recruit the top people in every field for decades. Scientists wanted to come work at Merck."

EPILOGUE

For many people the response to the question, "what is a leader" would be "some other person." The fact is that few of us think of ourselves as leaders. Harry Truman, who became one of this nation's great presidents, was one of those people. During World War I, Truman was just another doughboy, a soldier fighting in Europe. One night his platoon rode on horseback when German artillery shells began dropping nearby. Panic took over, and the men raced for cover. Truman's horse was hit and fell on top of him. Somehow Truman managed to crawl out from beneath the horse and, instead of retreating, he stood up and began shouting at the troops, ordering the men to get back into formation. The men were astonished, probably no more than Truman himself, who, until that time, had not considered himself to be a leader—but they listened to him. At that moment they were desperate for the leadership that he provided. Later, Truman wrote in his diary, "I learned two things about myself that night. First, I had a little courage. And two, I liked to lead others."

Like Truman, many of us discover we are leaders by chance rather than choice. We find ourselves in a situation the requires stepping up—and we do. Admittedly for most of us it usually doesn't involve being bombarded by artillery. Warren Bennis, the author of the classic *On Becoming a Leader,* and a man who has spent his life studying and lecturing about this topic, wrote, "No leader sets out to be a leader. People set out to live their lives, expressing themselves fully. When that expression is of value, they become leaders. So the point is not to become a leader. The point is to become yourself, to use

yourself completely—all your skills, gifts and ener-
gies—in order to make your vision manifest. You
must withhold nothing. You must, in sum, become
the person you started out to be, and to enjoy the
process of becoming."

Melissa Poe, the young woman who founded
Kids for a Clean Environment, stepped aside from
her leadership post at age seventeen to ensure that
the organization would always be run by kids. When
she was being honored on the twentieth anniversary of the founding of that organization, she reminded people:

**Change does not begin with someone else.
Change begins in your own backyard, no matter your age or your size. I had no idea that one
simple action could change my life so much.
Most journeys start this way, with simple mo-
tivation and a choice to do something or not.
You never know where the next step will take
you, and you never know where the next step**

will lead. The difference with being a leader is that you take the step; you take the journey. The greatest obstacle you will ever encounter is yourself. Just like Dorothy never knew she always had the ticket home, the Scarecrow always had a brain, the Tin Man always had a compassionate heart, even the Cowardly Lion had courage. Everything you need to be a successful leader you already have: Your intelligence to see an issue and a way to fix it, your heart to stay motivated, and your courage not to give up. You can't look for the man behind the curtain to solve your concerns. Everything you need you already have. It's all about taking the first step.

I asked at the beginning of this book for you to count the number of times you've shown leadership qualities in the last day. I suspect most readers found very few examples. Perhaps now you might have a different response to that question. I hope you have

Leadership is the ability to articulate a vision and walk the path so that you inspire others to rise above the banality and strife of their own common existence and achieve that higher goal.

learned that leadership isn't simply being at the front. It's possible for anyone to demonstrate leadership through words and individual deeds. It isn't what other people see you do, it's what you do in the quiet of your life that may later make a difference. It's the way you treat other people and the examples you set for your children. It's the simple kindnesses that may reverberate a thousand times, or the reassuring gesture that may provide the support someone needs. In truth, there are no boundaries for leaders; a leader can change the course of an entire nation or the life of one person at a time. Harry Truman and Luis Urzua became leaders because the circumstances in which they found themselves demanded it. But no one has to wait for compelling circumstances to become a leader. Leadership just as easily can be born of your own desires or your own desire to contribute, participate, or right a wrong.

There are countless definitions of "leadership." The Hall of Fame football coach of the Dallas Cowboys Tom Landry believed, "Leadership is a matter of having people look at you and gain confidence, seeing how you react. If you're in control, they're in control."

The former senator Bill Bradley, a member of the Basketball Hall of Fame, once said, "Leadership is unlocking people's potential to become better."

Permit me to offer my own definition of "leadership." Leadership is the ability to articulate a vision and walk the path so that you inspire others to rise above the banality and strife of their own common existence and achieve that higher goal. You can lead at many different levels. Being a leader often means seizing an opportunity or accepting a challenge. It may be as basic as volunteering to help in your child's school or at a local poverty agency; it might mean organizing a group to fight a neighborhood disturbance; for many of us it will be taking charge of a group in our work environment. You can be a leader in any area of your life.

We've discussed the ten tenets of leadership: listening; empathy; attitude; dreaming and making

Y ou are what your deep driving desire

is. As your desire shows your will, as your

will is, so is your deed; as your deed is,

so is your destiny.

—Brihadaranyaka Upanishad

decisions; being effective; being resilient; having a sense of purpose; demonstrating humility and humor; having integrity, ideas, and imagination; adhering to your principles, packing other people's parachutes, and demonstrating people skills. Put them all together, and, indeed, they spell "leadership."

The sacred Hindu text, Brihadaranyaka Upanishad, among the first of the more than 220 Upanishads, or philosophical statements, was translated into English in 1805. It reminds us, "You are what your deep driving desire is. As your desire shows your will, as your will is, so is your deed; as your deed is, so is your destiny."

In this book I have shared with you some truly inspirational stories. But none of us should ever forget that leadership is a marathon journey, not a sprint. Many of the women and men who have reached great heights started with a single small action. The Chinese philosopher Lao Tsu reminded us that, "A journey of a thousand miles begins with

Never doubt, that a small group of thoughtful, committed citizens can change the world. Indeed, it is the only thing that ever has.

—Margaret Mead

a single step." I urge you, if you haven't already done so, to take that first step.

So many of the leaders we revere were ordinary individuals who went on to achieve extraordinary feats. Margaret Mead, the anthropologist, once remarked, "Never doubt, that a small group of thoughtful, committed citizens can change the world. Indeed, it is the only thing that ever has."

There are countless examples of leadership that occur every day behind the scenes by individuals who don't seek or receive the fanfare of publicity. They lead in small and simple but exemplary ways, and they do it because it is their nature. But their contributions in making the world a better place are priceless. Leaders leave a legacy. They never strive to be legends.

Remember it is always possible to lead and that you can provide leadership in small or great measure. Leadership is a journey, not a destination, but the possibilities are endless.

As Søren Kierkegaard wrote in his 1843 book *Either/Or*:

> *If I were to wish for anything,*
> *I should not wish for wealth and power*
> *But for the passionate sense of what can be,*
> *For the eye which ever young and ardent, sees the possible*
> *Pleasure disappoints, possibility never*
> *And what wine is so sparkling what so fragrant*
> *What so intoxicating as possibility.*

Many of you, if not all of you, have already led, and have done so with great distinction. I invite you to take a moment and reflect on it; then go tell your story. Each one of you has the spark of leadership.

Now go ignite it.

SUGGESTED READING

The Art of Possibility, by Rosamund Stone Zander and
    Benjamin Zander
Authentic Leadership, by Bill George
Blue Ocean Strategy, by W. Chan Kim and Renée
    Mauborgne
Gandhi and Churchill, by Arthur Herman
The Leader Who Had No Title, by Robin Sharma
The Leadership Moment, by Michael Useem
Made to Stick: Why Some Ideas Survive and Others Die,
    by Chip Heath and Dan Heath
On Becoming a Leader, by Warren Bennis

Suggested Reading

Onward: How Starbucks Fought for Its Life Without Losing Its Soul, by Howard Schultz and Joanne Gordon

The Power of Ethical Management, by Kenneth Blanchard and Norman Vincent Peale

The Seven Spiritual Laws of Success, by Deepak Chopra

Team of Rivals, by Doris Kearns Goodwin

True North, by Bill George

The Truth About Leadership, by James M. Kouzes and Barry Z. Posner

Winning, by Jack Welch and Suzy Welch

Winston Churchill, CEO, by Alan Axelrod

You Don't Need a Title to Be a Leader, by Mark Sanborn

INDEX

Index

Index

Index

Index

Index